A Bullet from Heaven

Man's Lie or YHWH's Truth

Clifford Fearnley

A Bullet from Heaven

Man's Lie or YHWH's Truth

BY CLIFFORD FEARNLEY

2011

All scriptural quotations in this publication, unless otherwise noted, are taken from The Complete Jewish Bible by David H. Stern. Copyright © 1998. All rights reserved. Used by permission of Messianic Jewish Publishers, 6120 Day Long Lane, Clarksville, MD 2102. Some additional quotations have been taken from The Scriptures (TS) and The New King James Version (NKJV) and such passages are noted accordingly. Also the writer's clarifications or amplifications of verses such as Hebrew to English, have been inserted within the passage in parenthesis.

Cover art and design 'A Bullet From Heaven' by Shimoné Wolfaardt, New Zealand.

ISBN 978-0-473-19381-2

Clifford Fearnley is contactable via the websites:

www.undertorah.com and www.abulletfromheaven.com

Contents

Preface

> YHWH who has believed our report? And to whom has the arm of YHWH been revealed. (JOHN 12:38)
>
> And for this reason Elohim sends them a working of delusion, for them to believe the falsehood in order that all should be judged who did not believe the truth but have delighted in unrighteousness. (2 THESSALONIANS 2:11–12) (TS)

It has never been my intention to write a book, in fact, it was one of the furthest things from my mind. I am not an author and have never aspired to be. At the time this book was prepared I was a fully employed professional consultant working in an industry far removed from scripture. I can only say that YHWH (Yahweh) the Creator of the universe decided, for reasons beyond my comprehension, for me to be the pen in His hand. When I consider the subject matter of this book being the prophetic books of Daniel and Revelation, there is no doubt in my mind that the composition is His, I was merely the scribe. Most find these two books difficult and I am no exception. The book of Revelation in particular I have always found confusing and something of an enigma. Because I do not enjoy reading that which I cannot understand it has been an area of scripture I have tended to leave alone, visiting this section of the scriptures somewhat infrequently, waiting for what has now happened — for the message to be revealed.

There are many interpretations of the books of Daniel and Revelation available today and whilst some may achieve a level of credibility, the varied and generally conflicting information has, for me, just confounded the confusion. Should this book be considered any different? I would have to say it should, because of who the composer is. I can take no credit for the revelations contained within this book. At times the information for this book was fed to me in a somewhat staccato fashion which required a degree of personal application formatting the information as it was given. This would be my contribution. I would wake up from sleep in the early hours of the morning with a head full of information and would have to start writing. One thing I did learn, when YHWH wanted me I had to respond immediately if I didn't, the information was taken away from me. But I now realise YHWH has been grooming me for several years in preparation for this work. Over time He has fed me splinters of knowledge which are now encompassed within the content of this book. I hope your reading of this book will be an equally rewarding experience for you as working on it has been for me. As the meanings of images and phrases were revealed I have found the work exciting and fascinating.

Some may challenge, why would YHWH choose you? I have no answer to such a challenge but then why not? Messiah Yeshua selected ordinary fishermen to do His work. All I can say is, I have repeatedly given my thanks in prayer for being the one selected for this duty. It has been both rewarding and enlightening.

Even the title was given to me. I pondered a lot on this issue but just went around in circles. As you read your way through the contents you will, as I did, realise how appropriate the title is. For me it reinforces who the true author is but not only this, the title exactly portrays the book itself. It is clear to me that YHWH's intention is for this book to save souls but for those who reject its content, insofar as their salvation is concerned, it will indeed be as effective as a bullet to the heart.

This book reveals the meaning behind the many images described in the prophetic books of Daniel and Revelation. By so doing it unveils the thread of religious deceit that is entwined in all world society today and goes further than any other book I have ever read by exposing one of the greatest religious institutions and the administration behind it.

Clifford Fearnley

Introduction

In this book the following terms have been replaced as stated:

1) God replaced with Elohim. In places His name is used as instructed by Him in Exodus 3.15 but in the abbreviated form YHWH, pronounced Yahweh.
2) Lord replaced with Master.
3) Holy Spirit (HS) replaced with Ruach HaKodesh.
4) Sabbath replaced with Shabbat.

Neither is the Christian name Jesus Christ used but the name of the Jewish Messiah: Yeshua. The term apostasy as used in this book means rebellion against YHWH, the true Elohim, and the Creator of all things. To help the reader the initial changes are followed by the English in parenthesis.

To assist readers in understanding the message in this book, wherever the Hebrew word Torah is used it has been suffixed with (Law). However, contrary to popular belief and explained later in this book the Hebrew word Torah does *NOT* mean law. A more correct translation is teaching or instruction. In other words the Torah is YHWH's instruction for mankind. For those who are unaware the Torah is the first five books of the scriptures: Genesis – Deuteronomy, commonly referred to as the 'Books of Moses' or as just stated, 'the Law.'

We will be concerning ourselves with the books of Daniel and Revelation and we will be using them side by side. Anyone who has attempted to unravel the books of Daniel and Revelation will undoubtedly testify, that in addition to the difficulty understanding the information provided, there is the problem which arises from the convoluted manner in which the information itself is presented. In the case of the book of Daniel we can find some reasoning for this because Daniel was instructed to lock the information away, obviously until the time designated by YHWH for the prophecies to be understood. However, no such instruction was given to John with respect to the revelation given to him. Yet the book of Revelation is just as difficult to understand as that of Daniel, if indeed, not more so. But just as with the book of Daniel, so also has the book of Revelation required time for events to develop for its prophecies to be understood.

It is possible that the truth of Revelation has been kept hidden until YHWH decided to reveal what is written in 2 Thessalonians 2:5–11. First is the lie, then the truth followed by the delusion promised by YHWH for those who refuse to accept the truth and then judgement. The singular purpose of this book is to reveal to all, YHWH's truth and to expose the huge religious misconception mankind is currently suffering. In this book you will learn YHWH's truth and I plead with all who read it please do not turn away from it. Many will find the contents of this book unsavoury but don't condemn this book merely because you don't like what is said. The issue facing you is not an emotional issue it is a factual issue. Challenge these facts by all means but let the basis of your argument be the scriptures, not your love for your church or for the leader of your church. Judge this book against what is said in the scriptures. Just as any court judge would instruct the members of a jury, judge on the facts and nothing else.

A confusing aspect of the books of Daniel and Revelation is the many beast images given, even a woman riding a beast. Before we start it is important to understand that the scriptural reference to beast has of course nothing to do with animals. That is clear from the strangeness of the images described. Beasts in scripture symbolise apostasy, that is, opposition to the one true Elohim: YHWH. Satan is behind all of the apostasy permeating throughout the world and the beast images fully represent the workings of Satan within humanity by way of false religions (idolatry) and/or an unrighteous lifestyle. Any person following this form of lifestyle is worshipping Satan. There is no middle ground for humanity: it is either YHWH or Satan.

One aspect of difference between the beasts spoken of in Daniel and those in Revelation, is that the beasts in Daniel represent individual empires spanning millennia, each of which can be considered separately. The beast images in Daniel span from times ancient to the present and beyond, revealing the apostate condition of mankind. Whereas Revelation tells of the final development of the end time apostasy, which we will learn is occurring today and what will be its ultimate realisation. Each of the individual beast descriptions in Revelation is meant to provide different information about the end time kingdom and its leader, which is why each beast is slightly different. Collectively the beast descriptions in Revelation provide us with a complete picture of the characteristics and nature of the end time apostasy. There is, however, an overlap with some aspects with what is prophesied in Daniel which is why both books are referred to.

Revelation 13:3 says the whole world worshipped the beast. This verse should not be interpreted as referring to any one specific period or time. It is meant as a general statement of mankind's inherent willingness, since the time of its creation, to turn away from YHWH's Torah (Law) and instead, readily follow any form of false worship, generation after generation. Indeed, this verse in Revelation is just one verse in scripture that confirms what the beasts in Daniel represent.

A final note of difference between the books of Daniel and Revelation is that Daniel is particularly concerned with Satan's apostatic thrust against the nation of Israel. Whereas Revelation is more concerned with humanity's end time apostasy as a whole.

Together the books of Daniel and Revelation show how mankind has fallen away from its Creator, how the apostasy started many millennia ago, how it is present today and how it will remain until the return of Messiah.

Basically the information provided may be categorised in the following manner:

1) The woman riding the beast in Revelation chapter 17.
2) Daniel's beasts in chapter 7.
3) The first beast in Revelation chapter 13 verses 1–10.
4) The second beast in Revelation 13 verses 11–18.
5) The beast supporting the woman in Revelation chapter 17.

These categories have been divided into two groups: group 1 comprising 1, 2 and 3 above and group 2 comprising 4 and 5 above.

GROUP 1 – ITEMS 1, 2 AND 3 : These images are concerned with the historical developments of apostasy, its origins, its nature and what has become the greatest misconception of Elohim's truth. The beasts referred to in this group both come from the sea. The term sea has a specific meaning in scripture. Revelation 17:15 explains the term to mean peoples, crowds, nations and languages. This is a pseudonym for the whole of earth's humanity. In other words these beasts are borne of mankind.

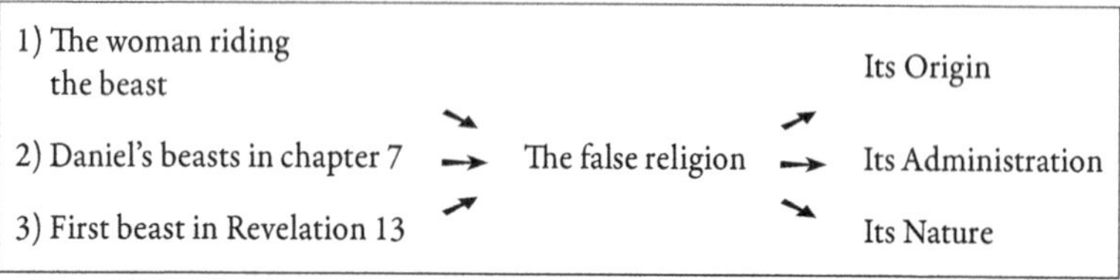

The similarities between the beasts of Daniel 7 and Revelation 13:1 leave no doubt that they are merely different images of the same entity. They all come out of the sea, both images are concerned with the pagan nature of the four separate empires Babylon, Mede/Persia, Greece and Rome. Both images had authority for the same period of time and both represent an arrogant speaking entity. The woman is associated with one of these beasts. As stated above these beasts are borne of mankind and the woman is a further representation of mankind's apostate attitude. The woman provides additional information concerning the nature of what the beasts represent. In essence, the picture provided in this first group of images portrays the working of Satan, from the time YHWH selected the Israelite nation to be His chosen people, up to the present day and beyond. This group of images merely precedes and overlaps the events to come as portrayed by the second group of images.

However, the connection between the beasts spoken of in Daniel chapter 7, the beast of Revelation 13:1 and the woman riding the beast is *limited to the little horn of Daniel and the pagan nature of the four empires symbolised by the four beasts Daniel saw.*

GROUP 2 – ITEMS 4 AND 5 : This group of images is concerned with events to come. As stated these images do however both overlap and supersede the images contained in the first group. The beasts referred to in this second group come up from the land. As with the term sea, the term land also has a specific meaning, this term is explained later.

4) The second beast in Revelation 13 5) The beast of Revelation 17	The man of lawlessness	The false messiah

Having said that the beasts of Daniel 7 and that of Revelation 13: 1–10 represent the same entity, as with every beast description in the scriptures, there are differences. One significant difference is the ten horns. It needs to be understood that the ten horns of Daniel chapter 7 have no relationship with the ten horns of the beasts in either Revelation 13 or 17. They each relate to a different time and event. It is important to recognise this fact. The ten horns in Daniel correlate with the ten toes of the statue in Daniel chapter 2. Both represent the fall of the Roman Empire: an event past. Whereas the ten horns spoken of in Revelation, we will see, refer to end time events which are yet to happen. As we have just said, only the little horn of Daniel is of any relevance to the subject matter of this book.

This book has been divided into four principal parts:

PART I – GROUP 1 : This first part examines how mankind has been whitewashed with the deceit represented by the images of this group and how the apostate nature of ancient times has been continued and will continue until the return of Messiah.

PART II – GROUP 2 : Deals with the end time spiritual force forming the delusion promised by Elohim in 2 Thessalonians chapter 2 and represented by the images in group two.

PART III – ELOHIM'S TRUTH : This section deals with several common misconceptions of YHWH's truth.

PART IV – EPILOGUE : Helpful verses and educational information.

NOTE: Before you start this book it is important for you to differentiate between those who follow a faith and the faith itself. It is not the intention of this book to condemn any individual or group. The primary concern of this book, is the false teaching that is misleading those who are genuinely seeking a proper relationship with the One who created them: YHWH. With very few exceptions, this book is wholly reliant on the content of YHWH's Word to sufficiently reveal the deceptive teaching prevalent throughout humanity today. As you progress through this book you will learn, not only was this deception prophesied but also the magnitude of it. The scriptures prophesy that the *whole* of humanity will be deceived; this statement *must* be taken literally. As you work your way through what is written do not let the enormity of the deception prejudice your view of this book. The deception has to be of a universal scale, to fulfil what the scriptures say. Therefore the deception has to be by way of one of the most common religious followings present today.

A BULLET FROM HEAVEN

PART ONE

PART I

The Universal Lie

WHAT IS THE LIE?

A lie is the opposite of the truth, so what is the truth? The truth is that YHWH is the one and only true Elohim, He is the Creator of the universe and all that it comprises. All is His footstool. The truth is, that He formed the nation Israel, through whom the whole of humanity would know Him. The truth is, He gave His Torah (Law) to Israel for the benefit of all mankind. The truth is, He sent His one and only Son, Messiah Yeshua, to be mankind's saviour and bring all of humanity under the umbrella of His Father's Torah (Law). The truth is, YHWH has never rescinded, reduced, annulled or changed His Torah (Law). This has always been YHWH's truth and it has never changed. Any form of worship, teaching or following contrary to these truths is a lie, a deceit and an abomination to YHWH. Today the lie is universal and is entrenched in society; this book will expose the lie and reveal how it has become so entrenched.

THE DIVINE WARNING

Revelation chapter 14 verses 9–10 provide the following warning:

> Another angel, a third one, followed them and said in a loud voice, "If anyone worships the beast and its image and receives the mark on his forehead or on his hand, he will indeed drink the wine of Elohim's fury poured undiluted into the cup of His rage. He will be tormented by fire and sulphur before the holy angels and before the Lamb."

This is singularly the most serious warning given in the scriptures insofar as mankind's eternal destiny is concerned. YHWH has given this warning because He does not wish for us to be deceived. But this warning would be useless if YHWH did not provide the information necessary for us to identify who or what these beast images represent. If we cannot reveal the message behind these images we cannot heed the warning and we will end up deceived.

Within this warning there are three prohibitions: worshiping the beast, worshiping the image of the beast and receiving the mark of the beast. To worship the beast means to follow Satan. A person is following Satan if he/she is not following Elohim's Torah (Law). This is the crux of life itself, there is no middle ground. *It is YHWH's Torah (Law) as given by Him to Israel at Mount Sinai, or it is Satan*. Satan is the master of lies. He is the one promoting all religious faiths not founded on YHWH's Torah (Law). Today many are unwittingly following a lie, believing they are worshipping YHWH when the truth is, they are worshipping Satan.

THE WOMAN RIDING THE BEAST

WORLDWIDE APOSTASY — THE EXTENT OF THE LIE

Since the original 'fall' by Adam, Satan has continuously and successfully led mankind away from YHWH. Indeed, it was because of mankind's rebellion against Him that YHWH chose the Israelite nation. Through whom He intended for the whole of mankind to return to Him. We will learn how, since YHWH formed the Israelite nation, Satan has relentlessly obstructed YHWH's plan for them and kept the whole of mankind in a state of apostasy (rebellion against YHWH).

The woman is described riding the beast in Revelation chapter 17. Later we will see how each of the seven heads of this beast was a tool specifically used by Satan against the Israelite nation at a particular point in time. We will see how the influence of pagan worship, also represented by the seven heads, is strongly active throughout, not just the land of Israel, but the whole world today and, according to the prophetic books of Daniel and Revelation, will remain evident until the return of Messiah Yeshua.

Here we will examine the woman and reveal exactly what she represents.

> Then came one of the angels with the seven bowls; and he said to me, "Come, I will show you the judgement of the great whore who is sitting by many waters. The kings of the earth went whoring with her, and the people living on earth have become drunk from the wine of her whoring."
>
> He carried me off in the Spirit to a desert, and I saw a woman sitting on a scarlet beast filled with blasphemous names and having seven heads and ten horns. The woman was dressed in purple and scarlet and glittered with gold, precious stones and pearls. In her hand was a gold cup filled with the obscene and filthy things produced by her whoring. On her forehead was written a name with a hidden meaning,
>
> BAVEL THE GREAT MOTHER OF WHORES
AND OF THE EARTH'S OBSCENITIES
>
> I saw the woman drunk from the blood of Elohim's people, that is, from the blood of the people who testify about Yeshua. (REVELATION 17:1–6).

Let us consider how this woman is clothed. She is dressed, in purple, scarlet and gold adorned with precious stones. Where else in the scriptures will we find a similar description of dress? It is in Exodus 28:

> "You are to summon you brother Aharon and his sons to come from among the people of Isra'el to you, so that they can serve me as cohanim, (priests) — Aharon and his sons Nadav, Avihu, El'azar and Itamar. You are to make for your brother Aharon garments set apart for serving Elohim, expressing dignity and splendour. Speak to all the craftsmen to whom I have given the spirit of wisdom, and have them make Aharon's garments to set him apart for me, so that he can serve me in the office of cohen (priest). The garments they are to make are these: a breast plate, a ritual vest, a robe, a checkered tunic, a turban and a sash. They are to make holy garments for your brother Aharon and his sons, so that he can serve me in the office of cohen. They are to use gold, blue, purple and scarlet yarn and fine linen." (EXODUS 28:1–5)

> "Take two onyx stones and engrave on them the names of the sons of Isra'el." (EXODUS 28:9)

> "Make a breastplate for judging. Have it crafted by a skilled artisan; make it like the work of the ritual vest – make it of gold, blue, purple and scarlet yarn and finely woven linen. When folded double it is to be square – a hand span by a hand span. Put on it settings of stones, four rows of stones: the first row is to be a carnelian, a topaz and an emerald; the second row a green feldspar, a sapphire and a diamond; the third row an orange zircon, an agate and an amethyst; and the fourth row a beryl, an onyx and a jasper. They are to be mounted in their gold settings." (EXODUS 28:15–21)

The woman is wearing a copy of the uniform YHWH commanded was only to be worn by the priests when performing their religious duties in the tabernacle. By her dress this woman symbolizes religious worship. But the woman is termed a whore, a prostitute, what does this infer? In Exodus 34:15–16 we are given the scriptural meaning of the term whore:

> "Do not make a covenant with the people living in the land. It will cause you to go astray after their gods and sacrifice to their gods. Then they will invite you to join them in eating their sacrifices, and you will take their daughters as wives for your sons. Their daughters will prostitute themselves to their own gods and make your sons do the same."

It says their daughters will prostitute themselves to their own gods. What YHWH terms prostitution is idolatry. It is prostitution against Him. So this woman who is riding the beast is duplicating what YHWH ordered to be worn by the priests serving in the tabernacle but she is a whore, a prostitute. She must therefore represent false worship. But this woman does not represent just one form of false worship, this is clear from her title: 'Bavel the great, mother of whores and of the earth's obscenities.' Of the earth's obscenities, this woman encompasses all forms of false worship throughout the whole of mankind. Look at what is said in verses 2 and 15 of Revelation 17:

> ... and the people living on earth have become drunk from the wine of her whoring. (REVELATION 17:2)
>
> Then he said to me, "The waters that you saw, where the whore is sitting, are peoples, crowds, nations and languages." (REVELATION.17:15).

We said in the Introduction to this book that the term 'waters' is a pseudonym for the whole of humanity. This woman is described riding the beast; inferring control, because she singularly symbolises how apostasy, in all its various forms, has completely subdued the whole of mankind. It is the prophetic picture of apostasy that is being described here. A victorious picture of how successfully Satan has led the whole of mankind away from its Creator, through the influence of false religious teaching in all its religious pagan forms.

The term 'Bavel the great' in this whore's title is a reference to the legacy left from the ancient city of Babylon. It is a reference to the mystery of Babylon that exists today by way of the many types of false worship around the world, this being the waters in verse 15. At Babylon, YHWH introduced different tongues, languages, thereby creating separation within humanity. Separation leads to individualism and it is this individualism that has led to the many different pagan religious followings around the world. It is YHWH's intervention and its legacy to which the phrase 'mystery of Babylon' refers. It is because she represents this legacy, being all types of pagan worship, that the woman is given the title 'mystery of Babylon.' Throughout the scriptures Babylon is always seen as representing opposition to Elohim. It could be said that Babylon is to Satan what Jerusalem is to Elohim. Although the history of Babylon is not the subject of this book, we need to recognise that this apostate city was built on rebellion against Elohim. Its inclusion in Revelation is confirmation that the universal spirit of false worship that Babylon represented, is not only as virulent via the different types of religion today but will remain so until it is brought to an end by the counterfeit Messiah. Note it is the counterfeit messiah that will bring an end to the different types of religion in practice when he appears and not Messiah Yeshua. 2 Thessalonians tells us that Satan's disciple stands in the place of Elohim, to be worshipped as Elohim. We are told that it is he and his cohorts who put away *all* other gods, that is, all forms of worship other than that of himself. We will see as we work our way through this book, that the counterfeit will adopt one of the current false religions and force it upon all humanity as the single universal religion with him at its head. This act is symbolised with the destruction of the woman by this counterfeit as told in the book of Revelation and discussed in Part 2 of this book.

If it is not Messiah Yeshua who will bring an end to the many forms of false worship but the counterfeit messiah this leaves the question, why did the rock, spoken of in Daniel chapter 2 and representing the return of Messiah Yeshua, not just break the feet of the statue but shatter the whole statue destroying all of the various forms of pagan worship it symbolized? One can be forgiven for thinking that this image means that it is Messiah Yeshua who brings an end to the false worship represented by the statue. However, what the total destruction of the statue represents is that, when Messiah Yeshua returns and starts His millennium rule, He also will institute a single form of worship but it will be based on His Father's Torah (Law).

> For out of Tziyon will go forth the Torah, the word of YHWH from Yerushalayim (Jerusalem). (ISAIAH 2:3)

Pagan worship with all its history (symbolised by the statue) will be removed from mankind and all of creation forever. But it is important to understand that there will be only one form of false worship when Messiah Yeshua returns; the single religion imposed on all of mankind by the counterfeit messiah, which is discussed in detail in Part 2 of this book. Nevertheless, as is explained later this single universal religion will have all of the traits of past pagan worship symbolised by the statue. Messiah Yeshua will remove the counterfeit with all of his following and bring to an end this last great apostasy.

THE ADMINISTRATION BEHIND THE LIE

THE LITTLE HORN OF DANIEL 7

In the Introduction to this book we said how in this Part 1 we would be considering the beasts of Daniel chapter 7 and the first beast of Revelation 13 that is, verses 1–10. We said these beasts are merely different representations of how Satan has and continues to influence and control humanity. In this and the remaining sections of Part 1 we will constantly be cross referencing between these beast descriptions and therefore using these two books of scripture simultaneously. It will help at this point to reveal that the little horn in Daniel is also one of the seven heads of the beast described in Revelation 13:1–10. This is one example of the convoluted presentation of the information contained in the scriptures.

Returning to the subject. As stated earlier the whole world is in a state of apostasy by following false religious teachings. Most of these teachings are honest in what they are but one in particular, symbolised by the little horn in Daniel chapter 7, is the most deceitful of all false teachings. It is for this reason that the little horn has been given particular attention in the scriptures.

Let us start by looking at the book of Daniel chapter 7:2–7:

> "I had a vision at night; I saw there before me the four winds of the sky breaking out over the great sea, and four huge animals came up out of the sea, each different from the others. The first was like a lion, but it had eagle's wings. As I watched, its wings were plucked off, and it was lifted off the earth and made to stand on two feet like a man and a human heart was given to it.
>
> Then there was another animal, a second one, like a bear. It raised itself up on one side, and it had three ribs in its mouth between its teeth. It was told, "Get up and gorge yourself with flesh!" After this, I looked, and there was another one, like a leopard, with four bird's wings on its sides. The animal also had four heads, and it was given power to rule.
>
> After this I looked in the night visions, and there before me was a fourth animal, dreadful, horrible, extremely strong and with

> great iron teeth. It devoured, crushed and stamped its feet on what was left. It was different from all the animals that had gone before it and it had ten horns."

This vision of Daniel was merely a different representation of the four empires seen in the statue in Nebuchadnezzar's dream described in Daniel chapter 2: Babylon, Mede/Persia, Greece and Rome. There is no need to dwell on the significance of each type of beast, it is suffice to say that the image was a correct representation of the characteristics of the empire it stood for. It had to be, otherwise the image would be meaningless. For example, the second beast was a bear which came up on one side and had three ribs in its mouth. This beast represented the second empire Mede/Persia (the chest and arms of the statue). It says it came up on one side, symbolizing the rise of the Medes first and subsequently the Persians. The three ribs in its mouth most probably represent the three directions of conquest of this empire: west, north and south as described in Daniel 8:4.

But why mention these empires in particular? Why not mention the Chinese Dynasties for example? History tells us they were certainly around at the time and had their own form of religion. The reason these particular empires are featured in the scriptures, is because these were the empires used by Satan in his attempt to destroy Elohim's purpose for Israel: that is, for Israel to be a holy (set apart) nation living under His Torah (Law) and to be the example for the whole of mankind. Each of the empires described in Daniel conquered the Israelite nation and influenced Israel with their own belief systems of pagan worship. For this study we need only be concerned with the fourth beast, depicting the Roman Empire.

There is much controversy over the identity of the ten kings represented by the ten horns on this fourth beast. Many have spoken on this issue and there are several texts available. All have different conclusions and each believes that the interpretation presented is the correct one. If this was a simple matter there would not be any controversy at all. The absolute truth is, we do not know the identity of these ten and ironically their identity is irrelevant to this prophesy: an examination of verse 8 of Daniel chapter 7 will clarify this:

> 'While I was considering the horns, another horn sprang up among them, a little one, before which three of the first horns were plucked up by the roots. In this horn were eyes like human eyes and a mouth speaking arrogantly.'

Daniel's attention was taken off the ten horns and he was made to focus on the little horn because the little horn was entirely different. It was this little horn that was to be the whole focal point of his vision. In verse 11 of chapter 7 it is only the little horn that is referred to.

There is however, a purpose for the ten horns being included in the image but it has nothing to do with who they were. To understand why the ten are mentioned we have to again look at the statue dreamt about by Nebuchadnezzar in chapter 2. The statue represented the prophesied conquests of Jerusalem and the land promised to the Israelites. The progression of these conquests was from the head to the toe of the statue. The ten toes represented the breaking up or fragmentation of the last empire: the Roman Empire. The prophecy was that the Roman Empire would not be succeeded by another single monolithic administration but the geographical area ruled by Rome would be broken up into autonomous states, each with its own ruler. This is why the toes are described as iron and clay, two very dissimilar materials, reflecting the different personalities of individual rulers. History confirms this prophecy. The ten horns in this beast image are synonymous with the ten toes of the statue. Their relevance is not in their identity but to provide the timing of the appearance of the little horn, that is, after the break up of the Roman Empire.

Because the ten horns are said to be ten kings (Daniel 7:24) most people, by extension, assume that the little horn must also be a king. It is sometimes thought that horns in scripture always represent kings; it is this verse in Daniel and verse 1 in Revelation 13 that are quoted in support of this argument. However, this argument ignores what is said in Daniel 8:22 concerning horns:

> As for the horn that broke and the four which rose in its place, four kingdoms will arise out of this nation, but not with the power the first king had.

Here horns represent kingdoms, not kings. Of course the two words kings and kingdoms are synonymous, you cannot have a king(s) without a kingdom to rule and vice versa. So in each instance we have to interpret whether the term horn is a reference to a particular ruler or to a kingdom which can span several rulers.

Because verse 8 of chapter 7 says the horn had the eyes of a man and a mouth speaking arrogantly, many consider this leaves no doubt that the little horn must be a king. But verse 8 does not call this little horn a king and we will learn that it does not represent a single ruler or king. If we are to be exact, neither does the little horn represent a kingdom but it does represent the equivalent of a kingdom — an independent sovereign state. The sovereign state represented by the little horn is a seed of apostasy, which is why it is associated with the four beasts in Daniel's vision.

The little horn is described as having a man's eyes and mouth because the sovereign state it represents will have a man at its head but he is not a king. This sovereign state is unlike any other in the world, also its leader is very different and quite unique; this will become very clear as we continue.

We said earlier that YHWH's warning would be useless if He did not enable us to identify the apostasy represented by these images. Well, YHWH does help us. He provides several clues for us to identify the little horn and we will see from the clues provided that the little horn does indeed represent the apostate side.

But why should the sovereign state symbolised by the little horn be given more attention than any of the other images preceding it? After all, the images given to Daniel and John in the book of Revelation, all represent the apostate state of mankind past, present and future. But unlike the teaching promoted by this particular sovereign state, most false religions are honest in what they are and the belief on which they are based. However, the religious system promoted by this sovereign state is as we shall discover, both deceitful and insidious.

Of all false religious teachings, only the teaching of the sovereign state depicted by the little horn claims to be based on the truth of the scriptures when, as we shall learn, it is not. It is because the very people being deceived, are those earnestly desiring a relationship with the one true Elohim: YHWH, that the little horn has been given particular attention in the scriptures.

So now let us examine the various clues given by YHWH that will help us to reveal the identity of the little horn starting with Daniel 7 verse 8:

1) In verse 8, firstly we are told that the little horn sprang up from amongst the other ten. In other words the sovereign state depicted by the little horn will establish itself after the collapse of this empire and from within the area where the ten kings ruled. The fourth beast represented the Roman Empire and Rome is in Europe, so it must be somewhere in this region. However, YHWH does much more than this, He tells us the exact location where this adversarial state will be.
2) Verse 8 also describes it as a little horn signifying it will be a small state.
3) Verse 8 goes on to say:

   > 'In this horn were eyes like human eyes and a mouth speaking arrogantly.'

   Here YHWH is telling us that this sovereign state will have a man at the head. This is nothing unique; each of the previous empires had its ruler. But for this verse to distinguish the little horn only in this way is an indication that this ruler will be quite different from all others.
4) Verses 21 provides another clue:

   > 'I watched, and that horn made war with the holy ones.'

5) From verse 22 we understand that this sovereign state will be in existence when Messiah Yeshua returns.

> '... Until the Ancient One came ...'

6) Our next clue is found in verse 24:

> 'As for the ten horns, out of this kingdom ten kings will arise, and yet another will arise after them. Now he will be different from the earlier ones.'

We have said under item 3 above, that the characteristics of the leader of this sovereign state will make him very different and as we have said earlier, this sovereign state itself is very different from all other kingdoms/states.

7) Verse 25 says:

> 'He will speak words against the Most High.'

This verse on its own is not clear and so we need to search elsewhere to find an amplification of the nature of the words spoken against Elohim. Revelation 13:1 will assist us. As we have said this beast is just a different image of the same end time entity as that portrayed by the beast in Daniel chapter 7. Revelation 13:1 tells us:

> '... and I saw a beast come up out of the sea, with ten horns and seven heads. On its horns were ten royal crowns and on its heads blasphemous names.' *Verse 5 goes on to say* 'It was given a mouth speaking arrogant blasphemies.'

Whilst Daniel says the little horn spoke words against the Most High, Revelation explains these words were blasphemies. Let us now clarify what scripture describes as blasphemous, let us turn to the book of Mark chapter 2 verses 5–6:

> Seeing their trust, Yeshua said to the paralyzed man, "Son, your sins are forgiven." Some Torah teachers sitting there thought to themselves, "How can this fellow say such a thing? He is blaspheming! Who can forgive sins except Elohim?"

Mark shows us it was considered a blasphemy for a man to claim to have the power to forgive sins. Only YHWH has the power of grace and be merciful for transgressions. In John chapter 10 verses 30–33 we have a further example of blasphemy:

> "I and the Father are one." Once again the Judeans picked up rocks in order to stone Him. Yeshua answered them, "You have seen me do many good deeds that reflect the Father's power: for which one of these deeds are you stoning me?" The Judeans replied, "We are not stoning you for any good deed, but for blasphemy — because you, who are only a man, are making yourself out to be Elohim."

So we can understand to blaspheme is also to describe ones self as equal to Elohim. So the man who is the head of this small state will claim to have powers equal to Elohim.

Returning again to Daniel 7

8) Verse 25 continues:

> 'He will attempt to alter the seasons and the law.'

9) Continuing further with verse 25, it says: that the set apart ones will be given into its hand for a time, and times and half a time. Here the phrase 'a time' represents a year, therefore we have here three and a half years. Again we see a correlation with Revelation 13 where, in verse 5, it says the beast power was given authority for 42 months. This clue requires further interpretation which we will examine later.

10) Revelation 13:3 informs us one of the heads of the beast appeared to have received a fatal wound but its fatal wound was healed and the whole of the earth marvelled after it.

11) Finally in Revelation 17:9 we are told that the seven heads are seven hills on which the woman is sitting.

For YHWH to provide so many clues, He clearly wishes for us to establish the identity of the little horn. But each of these clues has required its own time for fulfilment. In fact it has taken almost two thousand five hundred years for all of these clues to be fulfilled. This is the reason Daniel was told to lock away these prophecies. Obviously the images in the prophecies were meaningless until evolution provided the answers to all of the clues given.

THE IDENTITY OF THE LITTLE HORN

There is only one entity in the world today that satisfies all of the clues given by YHWH in the scriptures, that entity is Vatican City and the Papacy! Now let us see how the Vatican fits all of the clues given, considering the clues in the same order.

1) Well Vatican City is certainly in Europe.
2) Is it a small state? Vatican City covers an area of only 44 hectares. This is the size of a large park; even some small countries have farms bigger than this. Its population is only 1000.
3) The man at the head of the Vatican, the Pope, is certainly very different from all other leaders. Contrary to all other leaders, the Pope's only power is in the position he holds as the head of an administration of a religious faith.
4) Has Papal Rome ever made war against the holy ones? The term 'Holy ones' is not a reference to the messianic believers of today. We are considering historical not current events and this term is a reference to the Israelite nation.

   We are all aware of the crusades of Rome. The first crusade was called by Pope Urban II in 1095; its aim was to take control of Jerusalem. This resulted in the siege and capture of Jerusalem in 1099. The fourth crusade was called by Pope Innocent III who had the same ambitions as Pope Urban II.
5) Will Papal Rome be in existence when Messiah Yeshua returns? Well, we believe Messiah Yeshua's return is imminent and there seems no reason to think the Vatican rule is coming to an end. Indeed the contrary is true. The current Pope like his predecessor, John Paul II, is putting a big effort into

appeasing other religions so as to cement the acceptability of Rome.

6) Is the Vatican State different from all other countries and states? Absolutely. The Vatican is the only wholly ecclesiastical state in the world today. It is has no political base.
7) Is the head of this state; the Pope, guilty of blasphemy? Well we established that blasphemy is when a person claims to be equal with Elohim and claims to have the power of Elohim. Consider the following extracts from official Catholic publications:

A – LA CIVILTA CATTOLICA (THE CATHOLIC CIVILIZATION) :

This is a bi weekly periodical that was first printed in 1850 and has the full support of the Papacy. The following is an extract contained in the March 1871 edition:

> The Pope is the supreme judge of the law of the land; he is the vicegerent (replacement) of Christ, who is not only a priest forever, but also king of kings and lord of lords.

B – PROMPTA BIBLIOTHECA

The full name is Prompta Bibliotheca Canonica, Juridica, Moralis, Theologica, Ascetica, Polemica, Rubristica, Historica. Originally this was the work of Lucii Ferraris who was an 18th century Franciscan canonist. Since then there have been several revisions. This document has been edited and published by the Vatican and is accepted as the official Catholic encyclopaedia. The following are extracts from its content:

> The Pope is of so great authority and power that he is able to modify, declares, or interprets even divine law. The Pope can modify divine law, since his power is not of man, but of Elohim and he acts as vicegerent (replacement) of Elohim on earth.
>
> The Pope is of so great dignity and so exalted that he is not a mere man, but as it were Elohim, and the vicar (replace-

> ment) of Elohim. Moreover the superiority and the power of the Roman Pontiff by no means pertains only to heavenly things, but also earthly things and to things under the earth, and even over the angels, whom he is greater than.

A lot more is said about the Pope's authority and status in this publication. Incidentally, the Pope's tiara is a triple tiara. Could this be in recognition of his claim of rulership over the heavens, earth and below the earth?

C – CONSIDER THE BLASPHEMOUS NAMES GIVEN TO THOSE IN AUTHORITY IN THE CATHOLIC CHURCH:

- FATHER: Messiah himself told us not to call anybody on earth father,
- MONSIGNOR: This title means my lord,
- PONTIFIX MAXIMUS: Means greatest bridge builder. Who is the bridge builder between mankind and Elohim? Only Messiah Yeshua.

We will see later that in scripture a title is the same as a name. So is the Catholic Church taking the name of Elohim in vain?

8) Has the Vatican changed the law? It certainly has. The Catechism of the Catholic Church contains the following in respect of the Ten Commandments, see table on page 19.

The second commandment has been removed. Papal Rome has had to remove it because the Vatican and Catholic churches are festooned with images. We will deal with this issue in more detail later. To maintain ten commandments they have split the tenth commandment into two.

AS GIVEN TO THE PEOPLE ISRAEL		AS AMENDED BY THE CATHOLIC CHURCH	
NO	COMMANDMENT	NO	COMMANDMENT
1	I am YHWH your Elohim: you shall have no other gods before me	1	I am YHWH your Elohim: you shall not have strange gods before me
2	You shall not make for yourself a graven/carved image, or any likeness that is in heaven above or in the earth beneath or in the water under the earth.		Deleted
3	You shall not take the name of YHWH in vain.	2	You shall not take the name of YHWH in vain.
4	Remember the Sabbath to keep it holy	3	Remember the Sabbath to keep it holy
5	Honour your father and your mother	4	Honour your father and your mother
6	You shall not kill	5	You shall not kill
7	You shall not commit adultery	6	You shall not commit adultery
8	You shall not steal	7	You shall not steal
9	You shall not bear false witness against your neighbor	8	You shall not bear false witness against your neighbour
10	You shall not covet your neighbour's house, nor his wife his male servant, his female servant, his ox or donkey nor anything that is his	9	You shall not covet your neighbour's wife.
		10	You shall not covet your neighbours goods.

The Catholic Church, along with the majority of Christians, does not observe Elohim's designated weekly Shabbat (Sabbath). In the 'Compendium of the Catechism of the Catholic Church' in answer to the question:

> For what reason has the Sabbath been changed to Sunday for Christians?

The answer given is:

> The reason is because Sunday is the day of the Resurrection of Christ.

There is considerable controversy over the days of the week on which Messiah died and was resurrected. There are texts available today supporting a Wednesday, Thursday and Friday death, also a Saturday and Sunday resurrection. It is a topic that remains alive to day attracting much debate. Add the argument of how to calculate the beginning and end of a day and the correct meaning of the phrase 'beyn ha'arbayim' (between the evenings) and the controversy gains real momentum. However, these are very much separate questions and are not the concern of this book.

There is no scriptural reason to relate the weekly Shabbat with Messiah's resurrection. Neither did Messiah say that the seventh day principle set by His Father would be changed through His sacrifice. Whether or not Messiah rose from the dead on a Saturday or a Sunday, what authority has mankind to change that which is decreed by Elohim?

YHWH designated the seventh day of the week to be the day on which He is to be worshipped. But Christianity in general, not just the Catholic Church, has said, "we don't care what you (YHWH) have said, we will worship on Sunday." Some Christians may ask, "what does it matter on which day we worship so long as we worship?" It matters to YHWH, He set the seventh day principle when He completed creation and He himself rested 'on the seventh day.' In Genesis 2:2 we are told that it is the seventh day, not the first day, which Elohim blessed and sanctified.

Throughout the scriptures the number seven represents completion. It is the number around which Elohim has designed His whole sabbatical calendar. He has designated seven annual Festivals. In the story of Creation the seventh day, is the last day. A study of the creation record in Genesis will show that YHWH did twice as much work on the sixth day so as to rest on the seventh day. It was this principle He endorsed when providing manna for Israel in the wilderness.

Just as the seventh day completes the week and is a sabbatical (rest) day, so too is the seventh month a sabbatical month in which the last of YHWH's seven annual Festivals are held. Every seventh year was to be a sabbatical year for Eretz Yisrael (the land of Israel). The land rested, there was to be no planting or sowing for a complete year. After every forty nine (seven times seven) years came the 'Shanat Yovel' (Year of Jubilee). When any property sold due to poverty, was to be returned to its original owner and those Jewish persons sold into slavery were to be released. The fiftieth year was to be an additional Shabbat for the land. YHWH has allowed seven thousand years for the salvation of mankind. There are six thousand years of weariness and toil but the last millennium will be the sabbatical rule of Messiah who referred to Himself as being 'Master of the Shabbat.' The seven thousand years mirrors the seven day week, first, six days of toil followed by a day of rest: not a day of rest followed by six days of toil.

The first sentence of the fourth commandment says, 'Remember the Shabbat Day to keep it holy.' When we understand that seven, not one, is the sabbatical number in the scriptures, can there be any doubt that YHWH is referring to the seventh day. The day of the week which He blessed and sanctified. There cannot be two weekly Shabbats. In His Torah (Law) He is commanding all to obey that which He decreed. Is mankind at liberty to change what the Father Himself has decreed? Yet the majority of Christianity blatantly ignores YHWH and is content not to keep the forth commandment as meant by Him.

What may not be realised is that Sunday worship was common long before Catholicism and the Emperor Constantine. Sunday worship was common by the early second century. Consider the following abstract from the 'First Apology' of Justin Martyr (110–165 AD):

> "And on the day called Sunday, all who live in the cities or in the country gather together to one place and the memoirs of the apostles and the writings of the prophets are read ...
>
> ... Sunday is the day on which we all hold our common assembly because it is the first day on which Elohim, having wrought a change in the darkness, made the world; and Jesus Christ our Saviour, on the same day rose from the dead."

Amazingly, there are some people today who believe Sunday is the seventh day of the week — Monday being the first day of work. However, the two day weekend is a very recent (20th century) introduction into society. In earlier times people worked at least six days of the week. The words of Justin Martyr are clear that Sunday has always been the first, not the last, day of the week. Emperor Constantine gave Sunday worship recognition when, in 321 AD he introduced a law throughout the Roman Empire declaring Sunday to be the official day of rest. Subsequently, the Council of Laodicea (364 AD), which was a regional synod of clerics from Asia Minor, formally renounced the Saturday Shabbat and instituted the 'Lords Day' namely Sunday, as the correct day of worship for Christians. *Man has introduced his own commandment.*

Whilst church leaders understand that Shabbat worship spans a full day, most are quite ambivalent in getting this point into the minds of their congregation. Consequently, the majority of Christians follow an entirely different mode of worship to that commanded by YHWH in His Torah (Law). Remember the fourth commandment:

> "Remember the day, Shabbat (Sabbath), to set it apart for Elohim. You have six days to labour and do all your work, but the seventh day is a Shabbat for YHWH your Elohim. On it, you are not to do any kind of work – not you, your son or your daughter, not your male or female slave, not your

> livestock, and not the foreigner staying with you inside the gates to your property. For in six days YHWH made heaven and earth, the sea and everything in them; but on the seventh day he rested. This is why YHWH blessed the day, Shabbat, and separated it for himself." (EXODUS 20:8–11)

YHWH set apart a day, that is the whole day. From His command that no one whosoever not even livestock, do any kind of work on this day, it is clear that He is referring to a full day. The passage says that YHWH rested on the seventh day. It does not say He rested for about two hours in the morning, after which He went about his normal daily routine and then rested again for a further two hours in the evening. Attending church for a couple of hours at each end of the day and continuing life as normal in between, is not observing the fourth commandment in the manner intended. Such a mode of worship is contrary to the very principle behind a Shabbat day. Why would YHWH say do not do any work on this day? Because working takes our minds off Him. YHWH set this one day apart so that a person could meditate wholly on Him, without the everyday distractions and pressures of this life. On this holy day, YHWH is meant to be in the forefront of a person's mind every minute of every hour. Isaiah 58:13 leaves no doubt that YHWH intended a full day of worship:

> "If you hold back your foot on Shabbat (Sabbath) from pursuing your own interests on my holy day; if you call Shabbat a delight, YHWH's holy day, worth honouring; then honour it by not doing your usual things or pursuing your interests or speaking about them. If you do, you will find delight in YHWH."

And in Jeremiah it says:

> Here is what YHWH says, "If you value your lives, don't carry anything on Shabbat or bring it in through the gates of Yerushalayim (Jerusalem); don't carry anything out of your houses on Shabbat and don't do any work. (JEREMIAH 17:21–22)

When it comes to the extent of Shabbat observance the Prophets could not be more categoric. We are told that not only should we not be doing our every day things but we should not even speak about them. Whilst these words need to be understood in a correct context what is clear, is that we must put the world as far as possible from our minds for a *full* day. Sadly, there are even messianic congregations that perform poorly in this respect. More is said on this issue under 'Keeping Torah (Law) Today' in Part 3 of this book.

Continuing with clue 8: has the Catholic Church changed YHWH's seasons? Obviously we are not talking of the four seasons of the year, so what do we mean by seasons? Season in the scriptures means an event (explained later). Where and what are the events designated by YHWH in the scriptures? Leviticus chapter 23 lists the Feasts/Festivals of YHWH. In verse 1 YHWH makes it very clear that what He is giving are *His* designated times. These are to be the Holy days given by YHWH Himself. These are *His* seasons.

Let us look at Psalm 23 verse 3:

> He restores my soul; He leads me in the paths of righteousness. For His name's sake. (NKJV)

The phrase 'paths of righteousness' has been translated from the Hebrew 'be-ma'agalei Tzedek.' which means cycles or circles of righteousness. So a more accurate translation would be 'He leads me in cycles of righteousness. Cycles are events that come around repeatedly, so what are YHWH's events that come around repeatedly? The seven annual Feasts/Festivals He instructed in Leviticus chapter 23 together with *His* weekly Shabbat. These are the only circuits or cycles given by YHWH. Annexure 2 at the end of this Part 1 details the seven annual Festivals YHWH has designated *His* times and *His* holy convocations (events/seasons).

What the Psalmist is saying is that YHWH leads a person to righteousness via ma'agalei-Tzedek. In other words, observance of YHWH's cycles (His annual Feasts/Festivals), is the only means of achieving righteousness. But Papal Rome has done away with YHWH's only means of keeping righteous, His designated times, and replaced them with the traditions of man, Easter, Christmas, Lent etc. and Sunday worship, none of which can be found in the scriptures. Consider the decree of the Father in Deuteronomy 4:2:

> "... do not add to what I am saying and do not subtract from it." (DEUTERONOMY 4:2)

It should be noted that this command by Elohim Himself is repeated four times throughout the scriptures. But the Vatican/Papal Rome has selected to disregard this edict from the Father and in the words of Messiah Yeshua has added its own traditions as doctrines.

From where does the Papacy's belief that it has the authority to change YHWH's laws come from? Well firstly they believe that the Roman See, the Pope, is a descendant of the apostle Peter and that Peter was given a greater authority than the other disciples. This comes from a gross misinterpretation of Matthew16:13–19:

> When Yeshua came into the territory around Caesarea Philippi, he asked his talmidim (disciples), "Who are people saying the Son of Man is?" They said, "Well some say Yohanan the Immerser (John the Baptist), others Eliyahu (Elijah), and still others Yirmeyahu (Jeremiah), or one of the prophets." "But you," He said to them, "who do you say I am?" Shim'on Kefa (Simon Peter) answered, "You are the Mashiach (Messiah), the Son of the living Elohim." "Shim'on Bar-Yonah (Simon Bar-Jonah)," Yeshua said to him, "How blessed you are! For no human being revealed this to you, no, it was my Father in heaven. I also tell you this: "You are Kefa (Peter), and on this rock I will build my Community and the gates of Sh'ol will not overcome it. I will give you the keys of the Kingdom of Heaven. Whatever you prohibit on earth will be prohibited in heaven, and whatever you permit on earth will be permitted in heaven."

Let us just consider these verses:

Verse 13 makes it clear that Messiah Yeshua is addressing all of the disciples when He asks "who are people saying the Son of Man is?" Verse 14 does not say who provided the answer. Then Messiah asks them all another question "But you, who do you say I am?" This time it is Shim'on Kefa (Peter) who answers "You are the Mashiach (Messiah), the Son of the living Elohim."

Now look how Messiah Yeshua responds "How blessed you are." Who? Simon Bar-Yonah: "For no human being revealed this to you, no, it was my Father in heaven. I also say to you that you are," who? Not Shim'on Bar Yonah but Kefa (Peter). Why the name change? "And on this rock I will build My Community." The Greek for Peter is Petros which means stone or pebble and the Greek for rock is Petra which is an immoveable mass such as a cliff. What we have here is a Greek play on words, a Greek pun. But the Papacy has interpreted that Messiah is telling Peter that it is upon him alone that the kingdom of Elohim will be built. That he alone will have the keys of the kingdom and whatever Peter binds on earth will be bound in heaven and whatever Peter shall loose on earth shall be loosed in heaven. This interpretation suits the Papacy's desire for control over the Christian faith and is why they allege that all Popes are descendants of Peter. Consequently, it is alleged the Popes have the keys of the kingdom and whatever they do is automatically sanctified in heaven. However, not all of Christianity accepts this philosophy.

To interpret these verses in a manner that suggests Messiah Yeshua is addressing Peter only, is not only erroneous but nonsense because it contradicts what is said elsewhere in the scriptures.

In the above verses Messiah Yeshua is initially responding to the one who answered him — Peter, but there is absolutely no reason to suggest, as He continues, He is not referring to all of the disciples collectively. In fact, only by isolating these verses from other scriptures can such a misinterpretation have any credibility. Consider the following scriptures:

1 Corinthians 12:28:

> And Elohim has placed in the Messianic Community first, emissaries (apostles); second, prophets; third, teachers; then those who work miracles ...

It does not say first Peter, then the apostles, then the prophets.

Ephesians 2:20:

> You have been built on the foundation of the emissaries (apostles) and the prophets ...

It does not say built on Peter and the prophets.

Revelation 21:14:

> The wall of the city was built on twelve foundation stones, and on these were the twelve names of the twelve emissaries (apostles) of the Lamb.

Once again Peter is given no greater importance than the other apostles.

Then we have Matthew 28: 18–20 what the church calls the great commission:

> Yeshua came and talked with them. He said, "All authority in heaven and on earth has been given to me. Therefore, go and make people from all nations into talmidim (disciples), immersing (Baptising) them into the reality of the Father, the Son, and the Ruach Hakodesh (HS), and teaching them to obey everything that I have commanded you. And remember! I will be with you always, yes, even until the end of the age."

If only Peter has the keys to the kingdom, why is Messiah Yeshua instructing all of His disciples to go and build the kingdom of heaven? It is acknowledged there is a controversy arising from the Trinitarian exposé of these verses but whatever translation is used, it is clear the Messiah is addressing all of His disciples and not just Peter alone in these verses.

Finally, if Peter was to hold a greater position than the others, wouldn't Messiah Yeshua have said so in Mark 9:33–35 when the disciples were disputing who was the greatest among them? Messiah Yeshua simply tells them that the greatest shall be least. No special authority was given to Peter.

To suggest that Peter or any of the disciples individually is the rock upon which the Kingdom of heaven is built is completely unscriptural.

1 Corinthians 3:11 says:

> For no one can lay any foundation other than the one already laid, which is Yeshua the Messiah.

Messiah Yeshua's reference to rock in verse 18 of Matthew 16 is not a reference to Peter but to what Peter said in answer to His question, "you are the Messiah, the Son of the living Elohim." It is this knowledge and its acceptance that the Kingdom of Heaven is built on. Remember the words of Messiah Yeshua in Mark 16:16:

> "Whoever trusts and is immersed, will be saved."

In what are we to put out trust? That Messiah Yeshua is who He said He was: the Son of Elohim, the promised Messiah. It is this belief that the Kingdom Of Heaven is built upon. What is it we are to be immersed (baptised) into? It is into the authority of the Father, the Son and the Ruach HaKodesh (HS). To close this issue let me refer to Psalm 18:31:

> For who is Elohim but YHWH? Who is a Rock but our Elohim?

According to this verse if Peter is the rock he must be equal with Elohim. The conjunctive 'but' in the passage infers 'only.'

9) At any time in its history has Papal Rome ever ruled for only 42 months being 1260 days? The reader should be aware that the scriptures use a Hebrew calendar based on a 360 day year and not the Gregorian calendar of today. (The 360 day/year is an average but it is accurate, for confirmation the reader should research at WWW.360CALENDAR.COM). In scripture a day can represent a year and this is an example, so we have to ask has Papal Rome ever ruled for 1260 years? It certainly has. In 538 AD Emperor Justinian issued his decree establishing the supremacy of the Bishop of Rome, which is the Pope's official title. This started the prophetic period which ended in 1798 exactly 1260 years later. In 1798 Napoleon's general Berthier entered Rome and took Pope Pius VI prisoner and exiled him to France where he died in 1799.
10) The fatal wound was in 1798 when the French Directory ordered the end of the Papacy. However, the Papacy was restored in 1929 when Mussolini returned the Vatican back to the Pope and under the Lateran Treaty, Vatican City was established as a separate country. The head wound was healed.
11) With respect to the seven heads (Revelation 13:3) and seven hills (Revelation 17:9), the Vatican is in Rome and Rome sits on seven hills.

Only the Vatican satisfies every single clue given by YHWH in the scriptures to the identity of the little horn. But as shown above, Christianity in general is just as guilty of some of the same transgressions as the Catholic Church.

In establishing the identity of the little horn we have looked at the images from Daniel 7, and Revelation 13:1. In the Preface to this study we mentioned the similarities between the beast Daniel saw and that of John's revelation, let us just remind ourselves of these similarities:

- Both beasts came from the sea, that is, both are the product of mankind.
- Both beasts ruled for the same time.

- Both beasts continued the pagan practices of the four empires depicted. This is discussed further in the next section.
- Both beasts spoke in an arrogant manner against Elohim.

FOUR BEASTS IN ONE — THE FIRST BEAST OF REVELATION 13

(PAGAN WORSHIP IS PERPETUATED BY THE LITTLE HORN)

Of all the beast descriptions, the description given in Revelation 13: 1–10 has to be the most confusing because it is actually seven beasts (represented by the seven heads) within a beast. If we remember that apostasy is represented by beasts in scripture, this description is nothing more than an historical picture of how apostasy has developed via the seven heads and is present today via the head that suffered the fatal wound (Papal Rome). The beast itself carrying the seven heads is a picture meant to encapsulate the apostate condition of the whole of mankind — *the whole earth followed after the beast (verse 3).*

Let us again consider the statue in Nebuchadnezzar's dream. As we have previously said, the statue represented four pagan empires that conquered the Hebrew nation. In the dream a rock (representing Messiah Yeshua) destroyed the entire statue, inferring that Messiah Yeshua will bring an end to these empires. Yet these empires ceased to exist long ago, so what is it about them that Messiah Yeshua will bring to an end? We need to take two separate verses, one from Revelation and one from Daniel and put them together:

> "... And I saw a beast come up out of the sea, with ten horns and seven heads. On its horns were ten royal crowns and on his heads blasphemous names. The beast which I saw was like a leopard, but with feet like those of a bear and a mouth like the mouth of a lion. (REVELATION 13:1–2)
>
> As for the other animals, their rulership was taken away but their lives were prolonged for a time and a season.' (DANIEL 7:12)

Why are the individual characteristics of each of the beasts spoken of in Daniel chapter 7, all wrapped up in this single beast entity of Revelation: the mouth of a lion symbolising Babylon, the feet of a bear representing Mede Persia and the body of a leopard representing Greece. Notice the beast representing the Roman Empire is missing? Insofar as the beast representing Rome is concerned, only the little horn is of significance and we have identified the little horn as being a representation of Papal Rome. But why has this beast in Revelation all of the characteristics of past pagan empires and why are they still present in the end time prophecies of Revelation?

The answer is in the verse from Daniel and is contained in the phrase 'for a time and a season' This phrase also appears in 1 Thessalonians 5:1 where we are given something of an explanation:

> "Now brothers as to the times and the seasons, you do not need to be written to. For you yourselves know very well that the Day of YHWH comes as a thief in the night. For when they say, 'Peace and safety' then suddenly destruction comes upon them as labour pains upon a pregnant woman, and they shall not escape." (TS)

In 1 Thessalonians verse 1 Paul tells the congregation he is writing to, that they do not need to be written to about the times and the seasons. In the following verse he explains why, reminding them that the day of YHWH is a mystery. He then describes end time events which are to happen. In these particular scriptures from Daniel and 1 Thessalonians time represents a period and as we have said season represents an event.

What the verse in Daniel is saying, is that, although the rule of these pagan empires will pass, the pagan worship and beliefs practiced by these empires will continue for a definitive time and will end with a particular event. This event is the end time event referred to as a 'falling away' in the scriptures and is discussed in Part 2 of this book. This 'falling away is a precursor to Elohim's wrath and the return of Messiah Yeshua. In other words, the apostate nature of these beasts will remain and under the single religion imposed by the counterfeit, will subdue mankind until the return of Messiah Yeshua. Hence the rock destroying the whole statue in Nebuchadnezzar's dream and the reference in Daniel to 'season and a time.'

Let us consider the basis of pagan worship and we will see how it is continuing today in fulfilment of this prophesy:

- The basis of Babylonian worship.
- The basis of mother and son worship.
- The pagan origins of Christmas, Easter and Lent.

BASIS OF BABYLONIAN WORSHIP

The Babylonians followed a system of worship based on the solar system. It was the worship of the sun as the supreme god because it gave life, light and warmth. This system of worship spread throughout the whole of mankind. You will find the solar wheel present in almost all pagan religions and the sun disk in religious paintings everywhere. The modern term for this sun disk is halo.

When I was a child I was taught that all of Elohim's angels have their own halo but Elohim's angels have no relationship with the halo/sun disk. One of the questions in the Trivial Pursuit game is, 'what is the origin of the halo.' A part of the answer given is — it is pagan and un-Christian.

I would like to tell a story of a picture I used to have in my bedroom: It was a very colourful and an attractive picture, it was in my bedroom for over three years. Suddenly, for no understandable reason I started suffering from poor sleep and headaches. This went on for a considerable time and eventually it became so troublesome to me that I went to see my doctor. He did the usual thing and prescribed a phial of pills. But the symptoms persisted and I really started to think I was suffering from something serious. Then on one particular occasion I walked into my bedroom and immediately felt a headache developing but on this occasion there was something else. There was a definite heaviness in the room, something I had not experienced before, it was very sinister. For some reason and at the time I didn't know why, I walked over to the picture and stared at it. Do you know for the first time in three years I actually saw what the picture really was. It had a pagan temple, pyramidal in shape without any apex. As I studied the picture I noticed an effigy of the sun about half way up the structure. I had never realised any of this before but the picture depicted pagan worship. YHWH showed me the truth of the picture on my bedroom wall. Obviously I removed it and true to say I have not suffered the same way since.

The reason I have told this story is because the material items around us can have a direct influence on our lives. The second commandment says do not make a carved image of anything in heaven, on the earth or in the waters below. Look up the definition of image in your dictionary, it can mean a painting, carving or statue. We will say more on this later. Paintings are nothing less than images carved with a paint brush. Clearly the painting I had was displeasing to YHWH. I would encourage you to check your possessions and remove anything that you feel could have an adverse effect on your relationship with YHWH. If you're unsure about an item just get rid of it.

Coming back to the issue: sun worship was Satan's means of diverting worship from YHWH. Yet the largest sun wheel in the world is in St. Peter's square in the Vatican. The paving in St Peters square has been laid in a pattern identical to the sun wheel of Baal. At the centre of this sun wheel is an Egyptian obelisk. The obelisk was worshipped as the dwelling place of the sun god. But this is not just any old obelisk. The obelisk at the centre of St. Peter's square in Vatican City is an original taken out of the pagan temple of Amon in Egypt. Could there be any greater abomination to YHWH. The temple it was taken from was the biggest pagan religious structure ever to have been constructed: it was approximately 1.5 km x 0.8km. I have read that the sacred enclosure at the heart of this building would have been large enough to house several average European size cathedrals. Leviticus 26:1 says:

> "You are not to make yourselves any idols, erect a carved statue or a standing stone (pillar)...."

Moses reiterated these words of YHWH when he was addressing Israel in Deuteronomy 12:2–3 when he says:

> 'You must destroy all the places where the nations you are dispossessing served their gods, whether on high mountains, on hills,

> or under some leafy tree. Break down their alters, smash their standing-stones to pieces, burn up their sacred poles completely and cut down the carved images of their gods. Exterminate their name from that place.

These are the direct commands of YHWH. Yet Papal Rome cherishes an original pagan standing stone placing it at the very centre of a pagan sun wheel.

MOTHER AND SON WORSHIP

But Satan went even further with pagan worship. He introduced a mother and child philosophy into Babylonian worship. The Babylonians worshipped Nimrod who, when he died became one with the sun: he became a sun god. Nimrod left a wife, Semiramis, who claimed to have been divinely impregnated by the sun god and she had a boy child named Tammuz. So we have the counterfeit of Messiah's birth, albeit premature. But it was the mother with the god incarnate son in her arms that became the grand object of worship. She was called the queen of the heaven and became the object of universal worship. This mother and boy child worship spread throughout the pagan world: ancient Germans called her the virgin Hertha, Scandinavians called her Disa, the Egyptians Isis with son Horus, in India she is called Isi with son Iswara, in Asia Cybele and Deoius. Finally, in China we have Shing Moo with babe in arms.

Today Catholicism has the same pagan system of worship, they have simply changed the pagan mother and child to that of Mary and the god incarnate Jesus. The Catholic Church refers to Mary as the 'mother of god,' 'queen of heaven.' the same title given to Semiramis and the others named above. But Mary is not the mother of Elohim; Elohim was around long before Mary was born. Mary is mother of Messiah Yeshua's humanity, she is *not* the mother of His deity.

Catholicism also considers Mary to be an intercessor between humanity and Elohim. Nowhere in the scriptures is Mary given this authority. There is only one intercessor, Messiah Yeshua and He makes this very clear in John 14:6:

"... No one comes to the Father except through me."

Clearly Messiah Yeshua's own words prohibit any other intercessors.

CHRISTMAS, EASTER, AND LENT

CHRISTMAS : The 25 December was a date celebrated by pagans long before the birth of the Messiah. It was adopted by Christianity from the week long pagan festival of Saturnalia in an effort to make Christianity more acceptable to the pagans. Because the festival of Saturnia had nothing to do with religion, Christianity labelled the 25 December as the date of the birth of Messiah to give this pagan ritual a religious credibility. The Jewish Messiah, Yeshua, was born around the September/October period, (Refer to annexure 2 at the end of this Part 1)

EASTER : The title Easter is taken from the name of a pagan goddess who was known by several names in various languages: Eostre, Ishtar, Astarte and Ashtoreth are just a few of her names. Eostre was the goddess of the Saxons, Astarte was the most important goddess of the pagan Semites. She was the goddess of love, fertility and maternity for the Pheonicians, Canaanites and Egyptians. Her name was Ishtar in Babylonia and Assyria. Aphrodite and Demeter in Greece, Venus to the Romans and Artemis or Diana in Iona Ephesus. The pronunciation of some of these names is where the name Easter comes from.

In The book of Judges we see that even the Israelites abandoned their worship of YHWH to serve Baal and Astarte (Jdg. 2:13 & 10:6). So we can see that goddess worship, which became the foundation of Easter started centuries before the coming of Messiah Yeshua, and it has absolutely nothing to do with Him or his Father — YHWH. Once again a pagan tradition was adopted by the church to attract pagans into Christianity.

Even the timing of the Easter period does not correlate with that of the death and resurrection of the Jewish Messiah Yeshua, who was executed at the time of the Pesach (Passover) Festival. This Festival occurs on the same date of the Hebrew calendar every year as would be expected. Whereas the date on which the Christian messiah, Jesus, died, being tied to Easter, floats around the calendar; consecutive years show Jesus died on different dates. Is this not sufficient proof that the Christian theology of Easter, is nothing short of conjecture forced on all Christians by Church leaders and teachers?

LENT : Lent is a forty day period of abstinence preceding the Easter celebration observed by the church. Where did it come from?

Cassianus a fifth century monk of Marseilles wrote the following about Lent:

> "The observance of the forty days had no existence in the early church, whence came this observance? The forty days abstinence of Lent was directly borrowed from the worshippers of the Babylonian goddess. Such a Lent is still observed by the Yezidis or pagan devil worshippers of Koordistan who inherited it from their Babylonian masters."

You will of course know that Ash Wednesday, another Christian following, marks the first day of Lent. For more information on how far paganism has influence the Vatican, the reader is encouraged to Google 'Pagan Sun Worship and Catholicism,' what you find will astonish you.

Adopting pagan practices and messaging them in a way to make them religiously acceptable is a transgression of YHWH's scriptures:

> Woe to those who call evil good, and good evil; who change darkness into light, and light into darkness; who change bitter into sweet and sweet into bitter! (ISAIAH 5:20)

> Indeed! Why not say (as some people slander us by claiming we do say), 'Let us do evil, so that good may come of it?' Against them the judgement is a just one.' (ROMANS 3:8)

Can there be any doubt that pagan worship (evil) is today being masked under the appearance of truth (good).

THE NUMBER 666

So what about the number 666? In Revelation 13:17 we are given three different characteristics that distinguish the beast:

1) His mark,
2) His name
3) The number of his name 666

It may be argued by some that 666 must be applied to a particular persons name and that this will help identify him as the Adversary. But 666 need not apply solely to a man's name because the same Greek word (onoma) translated as name in Revelation 13:17 is used in Revelation 19:16 where it is applied to a title. So Revelation 13:17 could just as correctly have been interpreted title. Today we address royalty and VIP's by their title. Their titles are used as names.

Prompta Bibliotheca states one of the Pope's titles is 'vicar of the son of god.' The definition of vicar is 'substitute for' or 'replacement of.' So the title, 'vicar of the son of god' means substitute for the son of god.

The title 'vicar of the son of god' in Latin is 'Vicarius Filii Dei.' Latin is the official language of the Roman Catholic Church.

VICARIUS	=	substitute for, or in place of.
FILLII	=	son.
DEI	=	god.

Roman letters each have a numerical value and when we calculate the Roman numerical value of these letters we have the following result:

V	=	5	F	=	-	D	=	500	
I	=	1	I	=	1	E	=	-	
C	=	100	L	=	50	I	=	1	
A	=	-	I	=	1				
R	=	-	I	=	1				
I	=	1							
U	=	5							
S	=	-							
Total		112			53			501	**666**

The Greek word for 'the Latin speaking man' meaning the Pope, is LATEINOS. Greek letters also have numerical values, which when applied to the word Lateinos also add up to 666:

L	A	T	E	I	N	O	S	
30	1	300	5	10	50	70	200	**666**

Whilst it is believed that the title 'Vicarius Filii Dei' is inscribed on the Pope's mitre and on his ceremonial triple crown or tiara, the Vatican argues as to the truth of this. The Vatican claims that there is no such title written on any tiara and that none of the Popes have ever claimed the title 'vicar of the son of god.' On the other hand there are available written testimonies from very responsible people. One of whom is alleged to have been a novice or practicing priest, who state that they have personally seen these words on one of the Pope's tiaras. One has to wonder why this controversy continues when it can so easily be settled. Let the tiaras in question be available for public viewing. But really these arguments are superfluous, unless the Vatican would deny the words spoken over each new Pope at his initiation ceremony. The crowning statement is:

> "Receive the tiara adorned with three crowns and know that thou art father of princes and kings, ruler of the world, vicar of our saviour Jesus Christ."

Would any Catholic argue that for them Jesus Christ is not their son of god? Isn't this oral statement sufficient confirmation of the 666 argument? Forget whether or not it is actually inscribed on a tiara, 666 is the title given to every Pope during his initiation. But the Vatican will probably deny this also.

If we accept that the Adversary is Satan himself, you can be assured the Pope is not the Adversary. Neither is 666 the number of the Adversary. It is however the number of the counterfeit messiah. So is it correct to affix the 666 title to Popes? The answer is very definitely yes because of the position both occupy and what they represent. The Pope is the head of the Catholic Church which is by far the largest division of Christianity, accounting for almost 60% of Christians. In reality this places Popes at the head of Christianity. In Part 2 we will see how the Pope occupies the very position the counterfeit messiah will assume when he appears on the earth and this is the essence behind the number 666. This particular issue is discussed further in Part 2 under the item 'More On The Number 666.' In Part 2 we will see that the title 666 has a specific meaning in the scriptures and Elohim has used the Vatican to expose its meaning. What is more, when we understand why it is included in the scriptures, we will see that by affixing this title to the Pope, the Vatican/Papal Rome is in reality defeating its own purpose.

CONCLUSION TO PART 1

In this Part 1, we have established the apostate nature of the little horn and how this horn was a prophetic picture of the Vatican/Papal Rome. We have learnt how the Vatican/Papal Rome has continued the doctrines of pagan worship and how it is decorated with pagan idols and symbols. We have seen how Elohim's scriptures have been distorted, manipulated and ignored by the Vatican/Papal Rome. How the Vatican/Papal Rome has drawn it's teachings, it's beliefs and it's doctrines from the pagan practices of the empires symbolised in the beast of Revelation 13:1–10 and disguised them as scriptural truths. Hence the pagan nature of these beasts has been kept alive in fulfilment of the prophesy in Daniel 7:12:

> ... but their lives were prolonged for a time and a season.

But the root of the end time apostasy extends well beyond the Papal customs of Rome. Whilst the position of Pope with all its traditions is an abomination, it is not the core of the issue described in the book of Revelation. The core issue is with the religion itself. Indeed, whilst Daniel chapter 7 via the little horn, targets Papal Rome, the story is far from complete and we have to understand that Daniel chapter 7 is merely a precursor to what is described in the book of Revelation. Papal Rome again features in the book of Revelation where it is symbolised, not as a horn but as one of the seven heads of the beast spoken of in Revelation 13:1–10. Specifically, it is the head that suffered the fatal wound. Although the problem prevalent in the end times may be seeded in Papal Rome, the following exegesis in Part 2 will show that the end time apostasy is not confined to the

Catholic Church alone but encompasses the whole of Christianity. We must not forget that Christianity is the foundational faith of the Catholic Church and that Catholicism is merely one of the many facetted faces of Christianity. Several of the transgressions raised above apply to the whole Church and not only to Catholicism. Part 2 of this book reveals how the path the counterfeit will ultimately tread has been well prepared in advance of his coming — under the guise of Christianity, not just Catholicism alone. Whilst Papal Rome is the catalyst used by the counterfeit to establish his authority: the following exegesis will reveal how the Christian faith itself is adopted by the counterfeit and forms the matrix of his final universal rebellion against the one true Elohim: YHWH. Part 2 elucidates how the counterfeit will assume the same position as the Pope, installing himself at the head of Christianity in fulfilment of the 666 prophecy.

The following Annexure 1 and 2 further demonstrate how the scriptures themselves are evidence of the dishonesty being preached today, not just within the Catholic Church but within Christianity itself. It is at this point I urge Christian readers not to put this book down but to continue with it. John 4:24 instructs that we must worship in spirit and in truth. If you are honestly seeking a proper relationship with the One who created you, it is imperative you learn the truth of what is in His scriptures. YHWH has given all individuals the gift of freewill. He has given all individuals the power of thought. He has provided each one of us with a mind of our own, it is now time to use these tools and for each individual to decide for him/herself what is the truth.

ANNEXTURE 1

The Appointed Times (Festivals) of YHWH

YHWH'S APPOINTED TIMES

YHWH's annual events are usually described as His feasts or festivals in most English scriptures. The English is a translation of the Hebrew 'moed' (plural moedim) but it is poor translation because moed more accurately means 'appointed time' or 'appointments.' So what YHWH is providing in Leviticus are the times of appointments which He commands all of mankind to keep with Him. The tabulation on page 42 details these annual appointments which He decreed are to be kept generation after generation.

In Leviticus 23:37 YHWH confirms that these seven moedim are appointments (seasons/events) to be kept as holy convocations. Throughout this chapter, YHWH makes it very clear that these designated times are memorials to be observed throughout all generations. As we have said earlier, these appointed times are the cycles of righteousness referred to in Psalm 23. Unfortunately most Christians consider this particular portion of the Torah (Law) to be a wholly Jewish affair.

Whilst the annual moedim are a separate study, it is important for the reader to understand that they are all *prophesies of Messiah Himself* through whom YHWH will restore humanity. With His death, resurrection and ascension up to heaven, Messiah Yeshua has fulfilled (not annulled) the first four of these events. Eventually but not until the end of His millennium rule, *when all will be complete*, will Messiah Yeshua fulfil all seven of YHWH's annual moedim.

NO	MOED/FESTIVAL		ACTIVITY	ASSOCIATED SCRIPTURE
	HEBREW	ENGLISH		
1	Pesach	Passover	Eating the pesach lamb	Exodus 12:1–14 & Leviticus 23:4–8
2	Matzah	Unleavened Bread	7 days without leaven	Exodus 12:1–20 & Leviticus 23:4–8
3	First Fruits	First Fruits	Waving of the sheaf of the first harvest: the barley harvest	Leviticus 23:9–14
4	Shavuot	Pentecost	Counting of the Omer — 50 days. On the fiftieth day another waving of first fruits this time of the wheat harvest.	Leviticus 23:15–22
5	Yom Teruah	Trumpets	Blowing of the trumpet	Leviticus 23:23–25
6	Yom Kippur	Day of Atonement	Burnt offering and sin offering by the high priest	Leviticus 16:1–34 & 23:26–32
7	Sukkot	Tabernacles	Living in booths (flimsy structures) for 7 days and rejoicing before Elohim. The eight day being a special Sabbath.	Leviticus 23:33–43

Considering the moedim are all blue prints of Messiah Yeshua, when we celebrate these events we are also celebrating the Messianic Vision, which explains Yeshua in very unique ways. The moedim represent the seven steps YHWH's has set for the redemption of mankind, which is ultimately achieved through Messiah Yeshua. When these events are understood in these terms, it makes no sense to say that they are for the Jewish people only. That is the same as saying that the Messiah Himself is for the Jewish people only.

The Gospel records show that Messiah Yeshua observed the appointed times decreed by the Father and with this in mind let us remember what is said in 1 John 2:6:

> He who says he abides in Him ought himself also to walk just as He walked.

When it says 'just as He walked' it means exactly as He walked, that is, to emulate His lifestyle. If we desire to know our Creator we must recognise and obey His will for our lives. Remember Messiah Yeshua's words in Matthew 5:17–19:

> "Don't think that I have come to abolish the Torah (Law) or the Prophets. I did not come to abolish but to complete. Yes indeed! I tell you until heaven and the earth pass away, not so much as a yud or a stroke will pass from the Torah (Law) — not until everything that must happen has happened."

When Messiah Yeshua spoke these words there was no New Testament so He had to be referring to the Tanakh (Old Testament). What Messiah Yeshua is saying is that He is the Messiah prophesied in the Tanakh and ultimately He will fulfil all of these particular scriptures.

FIXING THE TIMING OF YHWH'S APPOINTED TIMES TO THE GREGORIAN CALENDAR

To observe YHWH's appointed times we need to establish the start of the Jewish calendar that is, the first day of Aviv, this being the first month of the year. This is the base line for determining the date of each of YHWH's appointments. Each new moon sighted in Eretz Yisrael (land of Israel) marks the start of each month. For those of us residing outside Israel the necessary dates can be found on 'karaite korner' on the web.

ANNEXTURE 2

Calculating the Date of the Birth of Messiah Yeshua

THE CONCEPTION OF JOHN THE BAPTIST

The correlation between Elizabeth's, John's mother's conception and Mary's pregnancy, is the only clue available in the scriptures to calculating the time of Messiah Yeshua's birth. Even then we are unable to establish any exact date, only an approximation. But this approximation is quite sufficient to prove that Christianity's December date for their messiah, cannot apply to the Jewish Messiah: Messiah Yeshua spoken of in the true scriptures.

John the Baptist was conceived first and we need to establish the timing of his conception. John's father, Zacharias, was a priest and the first passages of scripture we need to consider are in Luke chapter 1:

> In the days of Herod, king of Y'hudah, there was a cohen (priest) named Z'kharyah (Zacharias) who belonged to the Aviyah division. His wife was a descendant of Aharon and her name was Elisheva (Elizabeth). (LUKE 1:5)
>
> One time when Z'kharyah was fulfilling his duties as cohen during his division's period of service before Elohim. (LUKE1:8)
>
> When there appeared to him an angel of YHWH standing to the right of the incense alter. (LUKE 1:11)
>
> But the angel said to him, "Don't be afraid, Z'kharyah, because your prayer has been heard. Your wife Elisheva will bear you a son and you are to name him Yohanan (John). (LUKE1:13)

> When his period of his temple service was over, he returned home. Following this, Elisheva his wife conceived ... (LUKE 1:23–24).

We are told that when Zacharias returned home from temple service his wife Elizabeth conceived. To establish the time of her conception we need to identify when Zacharias was on duty at the temple and from this, when he returned home.

The order in which the priestly families of the tribe of Levi performed their duties is given in 1 Chronicles 24:7–19. In all there were 24 'courses' and each would minister for one week twice a year in rotation. The order of rotation of service as given in 1 Chronicles 24:7–19 is:

NO	COURSE	NO	COURSE	NO	COURSE
1	Y'hoyariv	2	Y'da'yah	3	Harim
4	S'orim	5	Malkiyah	6	Miyamin
7	Hakotz	8	Aviyah	9	Yeshua
10	Sh'khanyahu	11	Elyashiv	12	Yakim
13	Hupah	14	Yeshev'av	15	Bilgah
16	Immer	17	Hezir	18	HaPitzetz
19	P'tachyah	20	Yechezk'el	21	Yakhin
22	Gamul	23	D'layahu	24	Ma'azyahu

The rotation was interrupted three times a year at Pesach (Passover), Shavuot (Pentecost) and Sukkot (Tabernacles), when all of the Israelite men were commanded by YHWH to travel to Jerusalem to celebrate each of these three Festivals. On these occasions it was necessary for all of the priests to be in attendance at the temple to accommodate the crowds. The effect of each of these Festivals was to push the rotation of the priestly temple duty one week further down the calendar. Zacharias was of the family Aviyah which was the eighth 'course' in rotation. Because two of the three Festivals, Pesach and Shavuot, would have interfered with Zacharias' rotation it is most probable that he did not return home until the end of the tenth week, around the middle of Sivan.

The following tabulation provides a comparison between the Gregorian (Civil) calendar and the Hebrew calendar. Unlike the Gregorian calendar the Hebrew calendar is based on lunar months, which as you can see are of a shorter duration. As a point of interest the Israelites were never meant to name the months of the year, YHWH gave the months numbers not names. The names adopted by the Hebrews are Babylonian names which the exiles brought back with them from their Babylonian exile:

NO	HEBREW	LENGTH (DAYS)	GREGORIAN
1	Nissan	30	Mar/Apr
2	Iyar	29	Apr/May
3	Sivan	30	May/June
4	Tammuz	29	June/July
5	Av	30	July/Aug
6	Elul	29	Aug/Sept
7	Tishri	30	Sept/Oct
8	Cheshvan	29/30	Oct/Nov
9	Kislev	29/30	Nov/Dec
10	Tevet	29	Dec/Jan
11	Shevat	30	Jan/Feb
12	Adar	29	Feb/Mar

From the above Elizabeth's conception would have been around the middle of the month of Sivan: May/June, probably early June.

THE CONCEPTION OF JEWISH MESSIAH, YESHUA

Now let us extend the above information to the conception of Messiah Yeshua. Once again we need to study some additional verses from Luke chapter 1:

> In the sixth month, the angel Gavri'el (Gabriel) was sent by Elohim to a city in the Galil (Galilee) named Natzaret (Nazareth), to a virgin engaged to a man named Yoseph (Joseph), of the House of David; the virgin's name was Miryam (Mary). Approaching her, the angel said, "Shalom, favoured lady! YHWH is with you!" She was deeply troubled by his words and wondered what kind of greeting this might be. The angel said to her, "Don't be afraid, Miryam, for you have found favour with Elohim. Look! You will become pregnant, you will give birth to a son and you are to name him Yeshua. (LUKE 1:26–31)

> "You have a relative, Elisheva (Elizabeth), who is an old woman; and everyone says she is barren. But she has conceived a son and is six months pregnant" (LUKE 1:36)

> Without delay, Miryam (Mary) set out and hurried to the town in the hill country of Yehudah (Judah) where Z'kharyah (Zacharias) lived, entered his house and greeted Elisheva (Elizabeth). When Elisheva heard Miryam's, greeting the baby in her womb stirred. (LUKE 1:39–41)

> Miryam stayed with Elishava for about three months and then returned home. The time arrived for Elisheva to have her baby, and she gave birth to a son. (LUKE 1:56–57)

From the sequence of these verses it is clear that the periods stated refer to Elizabeth's pregnancy. The verses put Mary's conception six months after that of Elizabeth. This places Mary's conception in the Hebrew month of Kislev (Nov/Dec). It is no coincidence that the Messiah was conceived at this time because the 25 Kislev is the time of the Jewish festival 'Hanukkah' referred to as the 'Festival of Lights.' Messiah Yeshua is referred to as the 'light of the world.' (John 8:12).

Since a full pregnancy term is approximately nine to ten lunar months, this would put Messiah Yeshua's birth in the month of Tishri (Sept/Oct). This is the time for the Festival of Tabernacles being the last of the three Festivals, when all the men of Israel had to assemble in Jerusalem. This was the reason Mary and Joseph were unable to find any accommodation.

Whilst the scriptures do not provide sufficient information to calculate the exact date of Messiah's birth, what is provided is sufficient to unequivocally deny any December date. Insofar as YHWH's scriptures are concerned the 25 December date is as false as the pagan festival from which it is taken.

A BULLET FROM HEAVEN

PART TWO

PART 2

The End Time Apostasy & Elohim's Great Delusion

2 THESSALONIANS 2:9–11

> 'The coming of the lawless one is according to the working of Satan, with all power, signs and lying wonders and with all unrighteous deception among those who perish, because they did not receive a love of the truth, that they might be saved. And for this reason YHWH will send them strong delusion, that they should believe the lie. (NKJV)

THE BEAST SUPPORTING THE WOMAN:
REVELATION 17:6–18 & THE SECOND BEAST OF REVELATION 13

In the introduction to this book we said how these two beasts came from the land. Together these two beasts represent the one end time entity that will lead mankind in a final rebellion against YHWH. We will see how this final rebellion will be centred in Jerusalem and will herald the return of Messiah Yeshua.

A) THE BEAST SUPPORTING THE WOMAN

Revelation 17:6–18:

> ... on seeing her, I was altogether astounded. Then the angel said to me, "Why are you astounded? I will tell you the hidden meaning of the woman and of the beast with seven heads and ten horns that was carrying her. The beast you saw once was,

> now is not and will come up from the Abyss; but it is on its way to destruction. The people living on earth whose names have not been written in the Book of Life since the founding of the world will be astounded to see the beast that once was, now is not but is to appear. This calls for a mind with wisdom: the seven heads are seven hills on which the woman is sitting; also they are seven kings – five have fallen, one is living now and the other is yet to come;and when he does come he must remain only a little while. The beast which once was and now is not is an eighth king; it comes from the seven and is on its way to destruction. The ten horns you saw are ten kings who have not yet begun to rule, but they receive power as kings for one hour, along with the beast. They have one mind and they hand over their power and authority to the beast. They will go to war against the Lamb but the Lamb will defeat them, because he is Master of masters and King of kings, and those who are called, chosen and faithful will overcome along with him."
>
> Then he said to me "The waters that you saw, where the whore is sitting, are peoples, crowds, nations, and languages. As for the ten horns that you saw and the beast, they will hate the whore, bring her to ruin, leave her naked, eat her flesh and consume her with fire. For Elohim put it in their hearts to do what will fulfil his purpose, that is, to be of one mind and give their kingdom to the beast until Elohim's words have accomplished their intent. And the woman you saw is the great city that rules over the kings of the earth."

We are told that John was altogether astounded by this vision and so in verse 8 the angel explains the meaning of the vision telling John:

> "The beast you saw once was, now is not and will come up from the Abyss; but it is on its way to destruction. The people living on earth whose names have not been written in the Book of Life since the founding of the world will be astounded to se the beast that once was, now is not but is to appear."

This beast will come up from out of the Abyss, the bottomless pit, whereas the beasts discussed in Part 1, those of Daniel 7 and Revelation 13:1, both came from the sea. In the Introduction to this book, we learnt how the term sea is a synonym for the whole of earth's humanity and hence the beast that came from the sea must be a product of humanity. Because the beast with the woman does not come from the sea, earth's humanity, it cannot be human so it must be spiritual. As it comes from the bottomless pit it must be one of the fallen angels spoken of in 2 Peter 2:4:

> 'For Elohim did not spare the angels who sinned; on the contrary, he put them in gloomy dungeons lower than Sh'ol to be held for judgement.'

These are the only occupants of the bottomless pit mentioned in the scriptures. Now look at how Revelation 17:3 describes this beast:

> "He carried me off in the Spirit to a desert, and I saw a woman sitting on a scarlet beast filled with blasphemous names and having seven heads and ten horns.

The beast description 'seven heads and ten horns' is a confirmation of the apostate nature of this beast, it is the same description given to the dragon (Satan) himself in Revelation 12:3:

> Another sign was seen in heaven; there was a great red dragon with seven heads and ten horns.

However this beast from the pit is not Satan himself, because Satan is not imprisoned in the bottomless pit, this is clear from what is written in the book of Job chapter 1. Describing the beast as having seven heads and ten horns is meant to depict it as both spiritual and demonic.

The release of this demonic entity from the bottomless pit satisfies the description 'once was; now is not but is to appear.' This phrase refers to this fallen angel originally being present in creation, subsequently being taken out of creation and imprisoned in the bottomless pit and ultimately being released back into creation. This demonic entity is more fully explained in the section C below.

B) THE SEVEN HEADS OF THE BEAST

In verse 9 of Revelation 17 we are told that the seven heads are seven hills on which the woman is sitting. We established in Part 1 how this was a reference to the seven hills in Rome where the Vatican is located. However, this woman does not just represent the Papacy because we are told that the seven heads symbolise something more. Continuing into verse 10:

> ... also they are seven kings – five have fallen, one is living now and the other is yet to come; and when he does come, he must remain only a little while. The beast which once was and now is not is an eighth king; it comes from the seven and is on its way to destruction.

The beast description in Revelation 17:6–18 is extremely convoluted and confusing. We are told the seven heads collectively represent seven hills being Rome and the Papacy, whilst at the same time representing seven separate kings of which, as can been seen from the tabulation below, the Papacy is one. It is important to understand, the beast descriptions generally represent how apostasy has continued and evolved over several millennia. In other words the beasts represent apostatic evolution.

There has been much wild and varied speculation concerning the identity of these seven kings. We said earlier how the two terms kings and kingdoms are often synonymous in scripture. This verse is a good example. The seven heads represent those kingdoms Satan has used in his attempts to usurp YHWH's plan for the Israelite nation. That is, those kingdoms which have had and will continue to have in the future, an influence over the Israelite nation. They would be:

1 2 3 4 5	Egypt Assyria Babylon Mede Persia Greece	5 have gone
6	Rome	Is now — was in power at the time of John's revelation
7	Papal Rome	Is to come
8	False Messiah	Eighth king (Revelation 17:11)

In chapter 7 of the book of Daniel several of these kingdoms are described as beasts and Revelation 13:3 describes one of these seven heads as having suffered a fatal wound but recovered. We know from Part 1 of this book that this is a reference to Papal Rome. Revelation 13:14 describes this same head as a beast, thereby confirming it is an apostate entity.

As said earlier in this book, collectively the various beasts described in the scriptures represent the whole of Satan's rebellious activities in this world, in all their various forms past, present and future. In other words, the beasts represent the way in which Satan influences and controls mankind to achieve his aims. Of these seven beasts, six are now historical. Today Papal Rome is the current beast and the false messiah will be the last beast. Because each head was/is Satan's tool at a certain point in time, at that time that particular head was in fact the beast. Each was the tool used by Satan to keep Israel under the influence of paganism and away from YHWH's Torah (Law). By preventing the Israelite nation from fulfilling YHWH's plan for them, to be the example for all mankind, Satan has successfully prevented mankind from coming to YHWH and kept mankind in rebellion against YHWH.

As we have said six of these kingdoms/heads/beasts are now historical. Although the history of these six kingdoms/beasts is not the subject of this book, the following is a synopsis of how each of these kingdoms affected the nation of Israel, enabling Satan to keep Israel under pagan influence:

EGYPT : The plight of the Israelites in Egypt is common knowledge. Their lives under Egyptian slavery and YHWH's hand in bringing them out of Egypt are well documented in the first chapters of the book of Exodus. Associated reading: Exodus chapters 1–12.

ASSYRIA : After the death of King Solomon, his son Rehoboam took reign over the Israelite people. However, ten of the twelve tribes of Israel rebelled against him and they appointed their own king, king Jeroboam. This left Rehoboam ruling only two of the twelve tribes these being Judah and Benjamin. This rebellion divided the nation into two kingdoms: the northern kingdom comprising ten tribes and the southern kingdom comprising the remaining two tribes. Associated reading: 1 Kings chapter 12.

The northern kingdom is referred to as the 'House of Israel' or 'Ephraim' in the scriptures and the southern kingdom as the 'House of Judah.' Both kingdoms followed pagan worship and as a result the northern kingdom was captured by the Assyrians in 722 BC. The ten tribes were taken out of the land and dispersed throughout the Assyrian Empire. Associated reading: 2 Kings 17:1–12.

BABYLON : Most people are aware of Nebuchadnezzar, the Babylonian king. YHWH intended for the capture of the northern kingdom by Assyria to be a lesson to the two remaining tribes (the southern kingdom) and turn them way from pagan worship and back to Him. However, Jeremiah tells us that the Judeans did not learn but continued with their idolatrous ways. (Jeremiah 3:8–10). As a result YHWH allowed Nebuchadnezzar in 586 BC to conquer the land and take the last two tribes into captivity. Judah and Benjamin were in exile in Babylon for seventy years. Associated reading: 2 Kings 25:1–11.

MEDE/PERSIA : After seventy years in exile, during which the Babylonians were defeated by the Medes, the Mede king Darius allowed the Judeans to return to the land to rebuild the temple. Associated reading: the books of Ezra & Nehemiah.

GREECE : Under Alexander the Great, Greece conquered the Mede/Persian Empire and took control over the Promised Land in 333 BC. The story of the Greek conquest over the land of Israel is related in one of Daniel's prophecies. Associated reading: Daniel chapter 8.

ROME : The Romans conquered the Greeks and were ruling over the Israelite nation when Messiah Yeshua was present on earth.

PAPAL ROME – THE CURRENT BEAST : Remembering that the beast description given in Revelation 13:1 and that in Daniel chapter 7, are representations of the same demonic entity. We are told in Revelation, one of the seven heads had received a fatal wound which had healed. We know from Part 1 of this book that this is a reference to

Papal Rome and in the order shown in the table above, Papal Rome has to be the seventh king/kingdom/beast. Papal Rome was responsible for the crusades against Israel. It was during the crusades that the Jewish people were offered a choice: the bible (Christianity) or the sword. It is in memory of this persecution that today the cross is seen as nothing more than an inverted sword to some Jewish people.

There appears at first to be a problem with nominating Papal Rome as the seventh king/ kingdom/beast. Verse 10 of Revelation 17 says that the seventh king must remain only a little while and therein lies the problem. As we discovered in Part 1, Papal Rome was inaugurated in 538 AD and exists today, hardly a short period. But in the vision the head wound has healed and so we are considering the period after the head wound was healed, which was in 1929. Now most believers are united in the belief that Messiah Yeshua's return is imminent. So the post wound period for Papal Rome when compared to the period preceding the wound, will be short indeed. Remember that before the wound the papacy reigned for 1260 years. This current reign is likely to last only a tenth of that period. Hence the reference 'a little while' in verse 10. But is Papal Rome branded a beast (apostatic) in the scriptures purely because of the Papal system it promotes? Absolutely not! As was stated in the Conclusion to Part 1, as big an abomination as it is, the Papal system is not the primary end time issue. It is the faith it represents: Christianity.

In the Conclusion to Part 1 we were reminded of the integrity between the Catholic Church and Christianity and how Catholicism is merely one of the many facetted faces of Christianity. The whole of Christianity has *added* the same pagan traditions and *subtracted* YHWH's annual Festivals as has the Catholic Church, in violation of Elohim's decree in Deuteronomy 4.2, not to add or take anything away from His Torah (Law). Messiah Yeshua builds on this decree, warning of the effect of man's manipulation of the Torah (Law):

> "Their worship of me is useless because they teach manmade rules as if they were doctrines." (MATTHEW 15:9)

These words apply equally to Christianity's lawlessness today as to the Scribes and Pharisees He was addressing at the time. To manipulate the Torah (Law) is to confront the Father and to confront the Father is to confront Messiah Yeshua. The words of Messiah Yeshua in His rebuke of Satan when Satan confronted Him through Peter are appropriate here:

> But Yeshua turned his back on Kefa (Peter) saying, "Get behind me, Satan! You are an obstacle in my path, because your thinking is from a human perspective, not from Elohim's perspective." (MATTHEW 16:23)

We can take from Messiah Yeshua's words that what is of man is not of Elohim and is of Satan. With its man made traditions and transgressions against YHWH's Torah, to whom is Christianity leading people, is it to YHWH or is it to Satan?

Contemplate also Messiah Yeshua's words in Matthew 7:21:

> "Not everyone who says to me 'Master, Master,' will enter the Kingdom of Heaven, only those who do what my Father in heaven wants."

What is it that our Father desires of us? Paul tells us in Romans 2:13:

> "For it is not merely the hearers of Torah (Law) whom Elohim considers righteous; rather, it is the doers of what Torah (Law) says who will be made righteous in Elohim's sight."

Only the doers of YHWH's Torah (Law), that is Genesis – Deuteronomy, will He consider righteous. Do not these words of Paul concur with our interpretation of the word 'paths' in Psalm 23?

Let us again consider Messiah Yeshua words in Matthew 5:17–19:

> "Don't think that I have come to abolish the Torah (Law) or the Prophets. I have not come to abolish but to complete. Yes indeed! I tell you that until heaven and earth pass away, not so much as a yud or stroke will pass from the Torah (Law)."

In Annexure 1 the phrase 'but to complete' in the above passage was clarified. As stated in the Annexure, Messiah Yeshua was referring specifically to those verses in the Tanakh (Old Testament) which prophesied the coming of a Jewish Messiah. His subsequent comments leave no doubt as to the precise interpretation He wanted these words to have.

'Not one yud or stroke will pass from the Torah (Law),' could Messiah Yeshua be any clearer? In His own words He will not bring an end to the smallest part of His Father's Torah (Law). Is He not, in this passage, reinforcing what His Father has decreed in Deuteronomy 4:2? Whilst Christianity purports to be a faith based on obedience to YHWH's scriptures and the Messiah spoken of in those scriptures, Christianity is blatantly disobeying what both YHWH and Messiah Yeshua say in the scriptures. You cannot profess obedience whilst being disobedient, such is absurd. We said at the beginning of this book that any religious following incompatible with YHWH's Torah (Law) is an abomination to YHWH. How many Christian churches today abide by the rules in Leviticus 23? YHWH's scriptures have been polluted, not just by the Catholic Church but by Christianity itself. When it comes to transgressing YHWH's Torah (Law) is not the whole of Christianity guilty?

The Papal tradition of Rome, obscene as it is is not the issue in Revelation. It is solely because of its position as the *head of Christianity* that Papal Rome is described as the seventh, current beast in the scriptures and continues its presence throughout the book of Revelation. Ultimately playing a prominent role alongside the counterfeit messiah in the final rebellion against YHWH.

THE EIGHT BEAST – THE FALSE MESSIAH : The false messiah is discussed in detail in the following section.

C) THE SECOND BEAST OF REVELATION 13

Now let us consider the second beast mentioned in Revelation chapter 13:11–18:

> "Then I saw another beast coming up out of the earth. It had two horns like those of a lamb but it spoke like a dragon. It exercises all the authority of the first beast in his presence and it

> makes the earth and its inhabitants worship the first beast the one whose fatal wound had been healed. It performs great miracles, even causing fire to come down from heaven onto the earth as people watch. It deceives the people living on earth by the miracles it is allowed to perform in the presence of the beast, and it tells them to make an image honouring the beast that was struck by the sword but came alive again. It was allowed to put breath into the image of the beast, so that the image of the beast could even speak; and it was allowed to cause anyone who would not worship the image of the beast to be put to death. Also it forces everyone — great and small, rich and poor, free and slave — to receive a mark on his right hand or on his forehead preventing anyone from buying or selling unless he has the mark, that is, the name of the beast or the number of its name. This is where wisdom is needed; those who understand should count the number of the beast, for it is the number of a person, and its number is 666."

Revelation 13:11 says:

> "Then I saw another beast coming up out of the earth. It had two horns like those of a lamb but it spoke like a dragon."

We are told that this beast also comes up out of the earth. Once again this is a reference to the bottomless pit. It also has the characteristics of the dragon. This beast and the beast being ridden by the woman are one and the same. They are just different representations of the same demonic entity. But Revelation 13 provides us with additional information about the characteristics of this demonic entity. Here we are told it has two horns like those of a lamb *yet the verse does not refer to it as a lamb*. There is a reason for this, there is only one Lamb of scripture, Messiah Yeshua, and this is not Him. But it is a counterfeit lamb, a counterfeit messiah. To learn more about the characteristics of this beast/counterfeit we need to look at 2 Thessalonians 2:3–11.

Before we consider these verses in 2 Thessalonians we need to make a clarification. In these verses the word 'revealed' is used three times. Insofar as these verses are concerned 'revealed' has one of two meanings depending on its usage. It means either to be physically seen or to be exposed as deceitful. It is important to our understanding of these verses for the correct definition to be applied each time the word is used. For some it may become clear as we work through the verses but for those for whom it is not so apparent the following are the correct definitions:

- VERSE 3 : Here the word is used to describe the exposure of a deceitful nature.
- VERSE 6 : In this verse the word revealed is used to describe a release from hiding or captivity, in other words a physical appearance.
- VERSE 8 : In this verse the meaning is the same as for verse 6.

Some readers may find it easier to substitute the correct meaning in the verse instead of reading the word itself.

The following verses from 2 Thessalonians are taken from 'The Scriptures.' Now let us look at the verses themselves:

> VERSE 3 : "Let no one deceive you in anyway, because the falling away is to come first (Before the Day of YHWH) and the man of lawlessness is to be revealed, the son of destruction,
>
> VERSE 4A : Who opposes and exalts himself above all that is called Elohim or that is worshipped,
>
> VERSE 4B : so that he sits as Elohim in the dwelling place of Elohim
>
> VERSE 4C : showing himself that he is Elohim.
>
> VERSE 5 : Do you not remember that I told you this while I was still with you?
>
> VERSE 6A : And now you know what restrains,
> VERSE 6B : for him to be revealed in his time.
>
> VERSE 7A : For the secret of lawlessness is already at work.
>
> VERSE 7B : only until he who now restrains comes out of the midst (is taken out of the way).
>
> VERSE 8A : And then the lawless one shall be revealed,
>
> VERSE 8B : whom the Master shall consume with the Spirit of His mouth and bring to naught with the manifestation of His coming.

> VERSE 9 : The coming of the lawless one is according to the working of Satan, with all power and signs and wonders of falsehood
>
> VERSE 10 : And with all deceit of unrighteousness in those perishing, because they did not receive a love of the truth, in order for them to be saved.
>
> VERSE 11A : And for this reason Elohim sends them a working of delusion,
>
> VERSE 11B : for them to believe the falsehood.
>
> VERSE 11C : that they all may be judged (condemned) who did not believe the truth but have delighted in the unrighteousness.

Unfortunately the presentation of these verses in the scriptures does not help in our quest to understand the end time picture painted by Revelation. Consequently, as can be seen, some verses have been divided into parts. Also we need to re-arrange the verses into a more helpful sequence starting with verse 7a:

> VERSE 7A : For the secret of lawlessness is already at work.

The secret of lawlessness is already at work. One set of scriptures I use has the following interpretation for this verse: 'For the separating from Torah (Law) is already at work.' I think this is a more effective presentation of this passage because it says exactly what lawlessness is.

It was explained in Part 1 of this book that there is only one Torah (Law): the one given to Israel at Sinai. Not one yud or stroke of this Torah (Law) has been rescinded (Matthew 5:18). YHWH's Torah is the only means of maintaining a correct relationship with Him (Romans 2:13). This being true, if you consider the world today 99% of humanity has no relationship with YHWH. We have Islam. Hinduism, Buddhism, Sikhism, Baha'i and no doubt some others. The woman is riding the beast across the globe today. The mystery of Babylon is not just alive and well, it is thriving today.

YHWH of course, knows what the situation is; He knows that very few are keeping His Torah (Law). He also realises that there are some who do not have a relationship with Him, not because they don't want to have a relationship but because they are ignorant of the truth. He knows that many who desire to know Him are being deceived, being fed false teaching and unwittingly, they are being led astray.

Verse 7a is not referring to Islam, Hinduism or the like, none of these religions are based on YHWH's scriptures, His Torah (Law) and the basis of these faiths is open and honest, therefore there is nothing secret about them being lawless (Torah-less). Christianity however, alleges to have YHWH's scriptures as its foundation when in reality, it is a faith that encourages transgression of that which is decreed in YHWH's scriptures. Christianity is just as lawless (Torah-less) as any of the other false religions. But Christianity is working secretly because it operates under a misrepresentation of what it truly is, thereby deceiving its followers. Remember what is said in Revelation:

> 'One of the heads of the beast appeared to have received a fatal wound, but its fatal wound was healed, and the whole earth followed after the beast in amazement.' (REVELATION 13:3)

As we said in the Introduction to this book, this beast image is associated with the historical development of the worldwide apostasy and its continuance up to the present. It comes from the sea and is therefore born of humanity, it is not spiritual. This verse is not referring to the counterfeit messiah. We have shown how the beast described with the fatal wound is a reference to Papal Rome but Christianity is the foundational faith of Papal Rome, you cannot condemn the one at the exclusion of the other. Of all religious following today 33% of the world population are Christians, Christianity easily has the largest following with Islam a long second at 21%. Christianity can be found everywhere around the globe. It has encompassed every country and race, hence the phrase 'the whole earth followed after the beast' used in the above passage.

There can be little doubt that Christianity is an apostate religion when, as we will see later, with the assistance of Papal Rome, the counterfeit will adopt the position of the Pope as the head of the Christian faith. We will see later how Christianity will ultimately be forced upon everyone in the end days by the counterfeit messiah under his new administration in Jerusalem.

Of course all practising Christians are indeed genuine in their desire to know their Creator. As is said in the Introduction, this book is not condemning Christians, this book is condemning the teaching that is deceiving them. Christians need to realise what is the scriptural truth and challenged those who are teaching falsely. They can either accept what the scriptures say or they can continue to listen to church leaders and follow the Church with all its traditions, in disobedience to YHWH and in accordance with Messiah Yeshua's own words, never know Him.

YHWH has decided it is now time for the truth to be known. The truth is in this book. Whilst some will accept what is written in this book, many, as confirmed in the verses following, will neither want to know nor accept the truth.

Now let us return to the other verses of 2 Thessalonians chapter 2:

> VERSE 11C : That they all may be judged (condemned) who did not believe the truth but have delighted in the unrighteousness.
>
> VERSE 10 : And with all deceit of unrighteousness in those perishing, because they did not receive a love of the truth, in order for them to be saved.

The leaders of false religions continue to be as effective today as they were a millennia ago, if not more so. The truth has been whitewashed for so long and so effectively, that false beliefs and doctrines are now cemented into society. Such is the state of falsehood that, as indicated by the above verses, the truth itself will be seen as a lie and rejected. Some will reject the truth because it does not suit their lifestyle; society today has adopted Saturday as its day of sport. Incidentally, long ago Satan used man's appetite for sport to keep him in rebellion against YHWH and today is no exception. Apostasy is encouraged in children from the earliest of ages because parents are not prepared to forsake their children's Saturday sport, instead they find it easier to forsake YHWH and ignore His holy day. In YHWH's words, "They delight in the pleasures of unrighteousness." But this will not be the first time that mankind has either not listened to or accepted the truth; the words of the prophets were rejected by Israel. Messiah Yeshua Himself was accused of being demonic and insane for speaking the truth (John 10:19–20) and his apostles were tortured. The above verses merely confirm that history will repeat itself.

Now let us continue with more verses from 2 Thessalonians:

> VERSE 11A : And for this reason Elohim sends them a working of delusion.,
>
> VERSE 11B : For them to believe the falsehood.
>
> VERSE 5 : Do you not remember that I told you this while I was still with you?
>
> VERSE 6A : And now you know what restrains.

Verse 11a & b is a continuation from verse10. Because people have rejected this truth, Elohim will send them a delusion. But 2 Thessalonians does not tell us what this delusion is. However, having been told that the beast we are considering comes up from the bottomless pit. Consider Revelation 20:1:

> And I saw an angel coming down from heaven who had the key to the Abyss ...

Add the following verse 6a from 2 Thessalonians to the above verse:

> VERSE 6A : And now you know what restrains.

The one restraining is Elohim's angel holding the key to the pit. Clearly nothing can be released from the pit unless sanctioned by YHWH. We have learnt that this beast is a demonic entity and is a counterfeit messiah. This counterfeit messiah is the delusion promised by Elohim in verse 11a. When Elohim believes it is time for His delusion, He will instruct his angel to release this demonic entity from the pit.

> VERSE 7B : only until he who now restrains comes out of the midst (is taken out of the way). Parenthesis added

> VERSE 8A : And then the lawless one shall be revealed.
>
> VERSE 6B : For him to be revealed in his time.

Verse 7b refers to the one holding the keys no longer obstructing (no longer restraining) the release of this demonic entity and the reference to 'him' in verse 6b refers to the beast (counterfeit messiah) himself.

> VERSE 9 : The coming of the lawless one is according to the working of Satan, with all power and signs and wonders of falsehood.

Satan is the epitome of deceit and he will invest all of his powers in this counterfeit messiah, which is why this counterfeit is described as the dragon, Satan himself (having seven heads and ten horns).

Looking at verses 11a & b again, in several translations it says 'strong delusion' and not just 'delusion', and there is some justification for such terminology. It compares with YHWH's treatment of Pharaoh at the time Moses pleaded with him (Pharaoh) to release the Israelite people. We are told YHWH hardened Pharaoh's heart. What we have in verse 11a & b is YHWH adopting the same philosophy with those who have rejected His truth. They want to believe a lie, now YHWH will ensure that is what they do. He intends for His delusion to be strong enough to harden their hearts against the truth and encourage them to believe the lie. His delusion is really a punishment for those who have refused to accept the truth. Whilst verse 9 tells us that this counterfeit messiah will have all the power of Satan, we know that even Satan is subject to the authority of YHWH: refer Job 1:12 and Ephesians 1:19–21. In Revelation 13:13 we are told that this counterfeit messiah will even make fire rain down from heaven so as to deceive the whole world. Obviously such a fete as this will have to be sanctioned by YHWH. Verse 14 says he deceives the people living on earth by the miracles it is allowed to perform: allowed by whom? YHWH. Allowing the counterfeit to perform such great wonders as this supports the terminology 'strong delusion.'

So far we have revealed that this beast from the pit is a false messiah. He comes in fulfilment of the delusion promised by YHWH and comes with all the power necessary for him to successfully deceive everyone. There is however one significant difference between the counterfeit and the true Messiah. As we have learnt the counterfeit comes up out of the earth, that is, he comes from below. This is the opposite of how our true Messiah will appear. Messiah Yeshua tells us how He will return from Heaven above:

> "For when the Son of Man does come, it will be like lightning that flashes out of the east and fills the sky to the western horizon." (MATTHEW 24:27)

When the true Messiah returns the whole of the sky will light up and it is this lightning in the sky that we must look for. This lightning must not be confused with the heavenly fire produced by the counterfeit. It is probable only those whose names are written in the Book of Life, (the wise ones Revelation 17:8) will be able to make this distinction.

We are now left with verses 3, 4 and 8 of 2 Thessalonians chapter 2 but before we can begin to understand these verses we need to first unravel some of the other mysteries of Revelation.

THE IMAGE OF THE BEAST

Let us now consider Revelation 13:14–15:

> It deceives the people living on earth by the miracles it is allowed to perform in the presence of the beast, and it tells them to make an image honouring the beast that was struck by the sword but came alive again. It was allowed to put breath into the image of the beast, so that the image of the beast could even speak; and it was allowed to cause anyone who would not worship the image of the beast to be put to death.

What do these verses really mean? Well let's see what they don't mean. These verses are not referring to a monument or construction of some sort. Whilst it says this second beast was allowed to put breath into the image so that it could speak, let's not enter the world of science fiction and think we have talking monuments.

These verses state quite clearly the image is to the beast that suffered a fatal wound; we now know that this is a reference to Papal

Rome. So the image honouring the beast is an image that in some way will be a credit to Papal Rome. But this is not a reference to the Papal system itself. In reality, Papal Rome is nothing more than an administration, it is the seat of power behind Catholicism and the head of Christianity. The revelation here is that the counterfeit messiah will create a new administration of his own, 'in the image of Rome.' It must therefore be a Christian administration acknowledging the achievements of Papal Rome. This point is discussed in more detail in the conclusion to this Part 2. Papal Rome and the counterfeit will work together. When Messiah Yeshua returns these two will unite against Him and ultimately they will be destroyed together by Messiah Yeshua:

> I saw the beast, and the kings of the earth, and their armies gathered together to do battle with the rider of the horse and his army. But the beast (Papal Rome) was taken captive, and with it the false prophet (counterfeit messiah) who, in its presence (The presence of the beast–Papal Rome), had done the miracles which he had used to deceive those who had received the mark of the beast and those who had worshipped his image. The beast and the false prophet (Papal Rome and the counterfeit messiah) were both thrown alive into the lake of fire that burns with sulphur. The rest were killed with the sword that goes out of the mouth of the rider on the horse. (REVELATION 19:19–21)

Parentheses have been added for clarity and are not part of the original text. The reader may have thought that the beast in the above passage was a reference to Satan himself but Satan's demise is described in the opening verses of the following chapter. Let us continue with Revelation 17:12–13:

> The ten horns you saw are ten kings who have not yet begun to rule, but they receive power as kings for one hour, along with the beast. They have one mind, and they hand over their power and authority to the beast.

To confuse matters, in these verses the term beast is referring to the counterfeit himself and not Papal Rome. Here we are told that the ten horns and the beast (counterfeit) are of one mind and that they act in unison. These ten are most likely other senior demons also from the Abyss. One of whom is probably the demon Abaddon, the commander of the demonic army described in Revelation chapter 9. It is with these ten that the counterfeit will set up his new administration. When the scriptures say the counterfeit puts breath into the image, this is a pseudonym for the counterfeit setting the policies and directions for this administration to follow. In other words he puts life into his administration, gets it motivated/working. The counterfeit is the head of this administration and will exert control over the whole of mankind through the ten kings forming his administration.

This counterfeit comes masquerading as the Messiah spoken of in the scriptures. He must therefore endorse a faith based on the scriptures. But he is a counterfeit, he serves Satan's cause. He is not interested in bringing people to YHWH so he has to use an alternative scriptures to YHWH's scriptures. The only alternative scriptures are the distorted scriptures of Christianity. The counterfeit's administration will actually encourage Christianity, which is why it is described as being in the image of the beast that suffered a fatal wound, (Papal Rome). Which explains the phrase, 'in the image of Rome,' used above. But why is a new administration necessary? Look at verse 4b in 2 Thessalonians:

> VERSE 4B : so that he sits as Elohim in the dwelling place of Elohim.

Most English translations contain the word 'temple' in verse 4 not 'dwelling place' as stated above. We are concerned with end time events and whether or not there will be a third temple at this time is a controversial issue and need not concern us. We are only concerned with the geographical location of YHWH's dwelling place, be it or be it not in a temple is not relevant to the issue before us. In Joel YHWH tells us He will dwell in Jerusalem:

> "You will know that I am YHWH your Elohim, living in Zion,
> My holy mountain." (JOEL 3:17)

Those who follow scripture are awaiting the return of a Jewish Messiah who will reign from Jerusalem. For his deception to succeed the counterfeit must appear to fulfil prophesy and must therefore locate his administration in Jerusalem. Verse 14 says everyone assists in setting up his new administration. Obviously there cannot be two controlling administrations and the following scripture confirms there isn't:

> It was allowed to put breath into the image of the beast, so that the image of the beast could even speak; and it was allowed to cause anyone who would not worship the image of the beast to be put to death. (REVELATION 13:15).

Here it says the counterfeit makes everyone worship the image of the beast (his new administration) and not the beast (Papal Rome) itself. The verses from Revelation 19 quoted above tell us that the beast, Papal Rome, will be destroyed by Messiah Yeshua when He returns along with the destruction of the counterfeit. So the legacy of Papal Rome must continue somehow but not in the capacity it enjoys today.

HOW WILL THE COUNTERFEIT MESSIAH PERFORM ON EARTH

We are told that this counterfeit messiah together with his associates (The ten horns/ kings) set up an image (a new Christian administration) in honour of the beast (Papal Rome). Together the counterfeit and his associates destroy the woman who rides the beast (bring an end to other forms of worship). They make everyone worship the image of the beast and ultimately, worship him (the counterfeit) as the head of Christianity. The counterfeit will force everyone into Christianity. But why impose a single apostate religion in place of several other apostate beliefs and followings? All false religions achieve Satan's desire to separate mankind from YHWH. So why impose a single universal false religion? It is because each religion has its own idol, its own god. The counterfeit comes in fulfilment of scripture so he has to represent the god of the scriptures. To achieve his desire to be worshipped as the one universal god he has to remove the opposition posed by all other forms of worship.

> VERSE 4A : Who opposes and exalts himself above all that is called Elohim or that is worshipped
>
> VERSE 4C : showing himself that he is Elohim

As we have just said, to succeed in his deceit, the counterfeit must fulfil the scriptural expectation of the return of a Messiah who is the Son of Elohim: YHWH. He has to take the role of the true Messiah who also will impose the one form of worship: that based on the Torah (Law) of His Father. This is confirmed in the book of Isaiah:

> Many peoples will go and say, "Come let us go up to the mountain of YHWH, to the house of the Elohim of Ya'aqob (Jacob)! He will teach us about his ways, and we will walk in His paths." For out of Tziyon (Zion) will go forth Torah (Law). The word of YHWH from Yerushalayim (Jerusalem). (ISAIAH 2:3)

This verse talks of the Gentile nations wanting to travel to Jerusalem, to Elohim's holy mount and worship the Elohim of Israel. Never has there been such a desire amongst the Gentiles to do such a thing as this. Neither has Elohim ruled from his holy mountain. This verse is prophetic: the passage seems to be referring to Messiah Yeshua's millennium rule and correlates with what is said in the end chapters of Isaiah. YHWH will teach us His ways through His Son Messiah Yeshua. Messiah Yeshua will ultimately remove the counterfeit from existence and end all worship of him. Messiah Yeshua will rule from Yerushalayim (Jerusalem) with a rod of iron (Psalms 2:9, Revelation 2:27), not tolerating any form of worship other than that of His Father's Torah (Law). For the counterfeit to succeed in his deception he must perform in a similar manner as is expected of the true Messiah and bring everyone to worship the scriptures but as we said earlier, not YHWH's scriptures, Christianity's scriptures

Let us consider how the counterfeit destroys all other forms of worship other than the worship of himself as the head of Christianity.

> As for the ten horns that you saw and the beast, they will hate the whore, bring her to ruin, leave her naked, eat her flesh and consume her with fire.' (REVELATION 17:16)

As we have said, the influence of Papal Rome continues in some form or other until it is destroyed along with the counterfeit by Messiah Yeshua. This confirms that the woman herself does not represent Papal Rome because she is destroyed by the ten kings.

The above verse could easily have said the woman is destroyed but instead it is quite graphic in describing her end; lay her waste and naked, eat her flesh and burn her with fire. Remember the counterfeit is allowed to make fire rain down from heaven. These graphic descriptions are meant to illustrate a time of great turbulence and tribulation. Mankind will not easily give up its religious followings and will rebel against the counterfeit, it will be a violent time. We know that Muslims for example, are very devout and extreme, they for one are not going to convert without putting up a very strong resistance. No doubt it will be the same for all other religions, the followers of each religion gaining strength from the resistance of the other. But their resistance will be to no avail because they are fighting that which is not of the flesh but which is spiritual. Those who continue to resist the counterfeit and his ten cohorts will be destroyed. The counterfeit will be merciless in his oppression. He will fulfil the scripture and will also rule with an iron rod. Not only will there be ethnic cleansing on a global scale as he puts down all other religions but Revelation 13:16 says, nobody will be able to do any business of any kind unless they follow the counterfeit. It will be a time of turbulence and difficulty like nothing before, but only for those who oppose the counterfeit, only they will suffer the tribulation.

WHO ARE THEY WHO WILL SUFFER THE TRIBULATION?

In Matthew 10:34–39 Yeshua tells us that even families will be divided with family members turning against one another:

> "Don't suppose that I have come to bring peace to the Land. It is not peace I have come to bring, but a sword! For I have come to set a man against his father, a daughter against her mother, a daughter in law against her mother in law so that a man's enemies will be the members of his own household. Whoever loves

> his father or mother more than he loves me is not worthy of me; anyone who loves his son or daughter more than he loves me, is not worthy of me. And anyone who does not take up his execution stake and follow me is not worthy of me. Whoever finds his own life will lose it, but the person who loses his life for my sake will find it."

These verses are worth developing. Messiah Yeshua is talking of the isolation that His followers are going to experience. Their faith in Him and their unwillingness to follow the counterfeit will cause them great strife, even within their family life. To the point that they will have to be prepared to forsake family.

Messiah Yeshua's words clearly show that He understands the magnitude of the difficulties that His believers will face. In these verses He is reminding us of His own sacrifice, His execution. In telling us to take up our own stakes and follow Him, He is telling us to be as resilient and unyielding in our faith as He was with the truth. Even if this means forsaking our own families and giving up our lives as He so willingly did for us. 'He who loses his life will find it.' That is, they will find eternal life. If, for the love of our family members, we forsake the truth and fall in line with those members who are following the counterfeit, in Messiah's words, we will not be worthy of Him.

Now let us look again at Revelation 17:8:

> 'The beast you saw once was, now is not, and will come up from the Abyss; but is on its way to destruction. The people living on earth whose names have not been written in the Book of Life since the founding of the world will be astounded to see the beast that once was, now is not but is to appear.'

In addition to those represented by the woman riding the beast: those following false religions, there are two other groups of people spoken of in the scriptures.

Firstly there are those whose names *are* written in the Book of Life, these are those who are destined for eternal life. Obviously these are the ones who have achieved righteousness in YHWH's sight. We have previously discussed the issue of righteousness and how to achieve it at length. We can infer from the above verse that Elohim's delusion is clearly not for them. They will recognise the counterfeit for what he is and will not be awe struck by his powers. These people too will show resistance to the dictates of the counterfeit. Many of this group will perish at the hand of the counterfeit. These are those who are martyred in Messiah Yeshua's name, refusing to follow the counterfeit's command to convert to Christianity. These are the ones described in Revelation 7:13–14:

> One of the elders asked me, "These people dressed in white robes – who are they, and where are they from?" "Sir," I answered, "You know." Then he told me, "These are the people who have come out of the Great Persecution. They have washed their robes and made them white with the blood of the Lamb. That is why they are before Elohim's throne. Day and night they serve him in his Temple."

When it says they came through the great persecution or tribulation it cannot mean physically because they have been martyred. What is meant is, they refused to give up the truth and succumb to the counterfeit. What this verse confirms is that even the righteous will suffer the tribulation, being the wrath of the counterfeit.

Finally, there are those who today are keeping YHWH's Torah (Law) but their names were never written in the Book of Life. These are the ones described as the seed that falls on rocky ground in the parable of the Sower:

> "The seed sown on rocky ground is like the person who hears the message and accepts it with joy at once, but has no root in himself. So he stays on for a while; but as soon as some trouble or persecution arises on account of the message, he immediately falls away." (MATTHEW 13:20–21)

Messiah Yeshua is not here referring to times past, He is prophesying. He says more on the issue of those who weaken in Matthew chapter 24, specifically in verse 12. When in answer to the question "What will be the sign of your coming and of the end of the age?" posed by His disciples, He says:

> "... and because of the increase in lawlessness (Torahlessness), the love of many shall become cold. But he who shall have endured to the end shall be saved." (TS)

'The love of many shall become cold.' In other words they will stumble when the going gets too tough and they will forsake their faith in the true Messiah. Nobody living today can consider they are already saved because nobody knows how well they will perform in the face of strong adversity such as will be experienced in the tribulation. It is clear from Messiah's words there are those living by YHWH's Word today who are going to fall away later on. It could be anyone of us. Only those who endure to the end are spoken of in Revelation 17:13–14 referred to above.

THE SIGNS OF THE END TIMES

The tribulation will be worldwide and will affect the whole of mankind, righteous and unrighteous alike. We know that the counterfeit is the cause of the tribulation but when will it occur? The scriptures are not specific in this but Messiah Yeshua has provided a clue in as much as He has told of the events which will herald the start of the tribulation:

> "Yeshua replied: "Watch out! Don't let anyone fool you! For many will come in my name, saying, 'I am the Messiah! and they will lead many astray. You will hear the noise of wars nearby and the news of wars far off; see to it that you don't become frightened. Such things must happen, but the end is yet to come. For peoples will fight each other, nations will fight each other, and there will be famines and earthquakes in various parts of the world; all this is but the beginning of the birth-pains."
> (MATTHEW 24:4–8)

We have reached a position where the world is never at complete peace. We now suffer continuous hostility in some form or other somewhere. Be it internal within a country by way of physical rebellion against its own government administration or the external aggression between one country and another or be it terrorism, which we now suffer on a universal scale. We have reached the point where our world is not without hostility for a single day of the year.

We are experiencing global weather phenomena without precedent, we have climate in chaos. The frequency of adverse weather being experienced today is unknown in history. Unmistakably we have already entered the 'birth pains' and are seeing these words of Messiah Yeshua unfold before our own eyes. If ever we needed proof of the truth of scripture, we are living through it today.

There are those who argue that the adverse weather conditions being experienced today, are the result of man's own failure to consider the effect his industrial advancement etc. is having on the environment and that the global weather condition has nothing to do with Elohim. Such an argument is probably correct, in part, but need not be interpreted as contradicting what is said in the scriptures. The scriptures provide many examples of YHWH using the natural elements to achieve His desires. The Egyptian plagues being one. There are many examples of YHWH using man's own nature to achieve His purpose. The warring nature of Israel's neighbours was used to chastise the Hebrew nation for their disobedience. Will the end times be any different? YHWH is using mans insatiable appetite for advancement, even at the expense of the environment, to fulfil that which is prophesied. After all wind, rain, fire, sea and shake are the very weapons in YHWH's armoury. He is the Father of all creation, all of creation is at His command, all is His footstool and available for His use.

The truth is, that the degree of hostility in the world today and the nasty weather we are experiencing, was prophesied by Messiah Yeshua. He warned that it would herald the beginning of the end time events described in the book of Revelation. Continuing on this theme, we can quote the following from the book of Daniel:

> "But you, Daniel, keep these words secret and seal up the book until the time of the end. Many will rush here and there as knowledge increases." (DANIEL 12:4)

The twentieth century saw an unprecedented rate in technical advancement. In just over a century, society literally went from the horse and cart to landing on the moon. Travel today is further, faster and more common place than it ever was. At the same time the electronic age became a reality, with the tiniest of components being capable of performing a multitude of processes in the blink of an eye. From the last century onwards mankind has certainly fulfilled these words in Daniel, which also herald the end times.

RETURNING TO 2 THESSALONIANS CHAPTER 2

We now have verses 3 and 8b remaining and we shall first look at verse 3 but before we do we need to clarify another issue. The tribulation and the 'Day of YHWH' are not the same thing. The tribulation is the result of the counterfeit removing all forms of worship other than that of which he is the head. 'The Day of YHWH' also referred to as Elohim's wrath, will immediately follow the tribulation but not until after the 'falling away' is complete.

> VERSE 3 : "Let no one deceive you in anyway, because the falling away is to come first (Before the Day of YHWH) and the man of lawlessness is to be revealed, the son of destruction.

Here we have a new phrase, 'falling away' which needs expanding upon because it represents an event of some importance; it is the precursor to the 'Day of YHWH.' We said earlier that today 99% of mankind does not have a relationship with YHWH. You would consider that whatever the phrase 'falling away' signifies has not only happened but must be as complete as it could be. However, we have to put this phrase into its proper context and we can only do this by considering the topic of the verses around it. In these verses Thessalonians is concerned with the end time events and in the context of these verses this phrase is an integral phase of these events. The verse links this 'falling away' to both the exposure of the 'man of lawlessness' and the 'Day of Elohim,' which we know are yet to happen. So the phrase as used in this verse, is prophetic and does not relate to mankind's current situation.

This book is about YHWH's truth. By revealing the truth, lies and deceit are exposed. People can only 'fall away' when they know the truth but are unwilling to accept it. But which 'truth' is the 'falling away' associated with. Is it the truth about Christianity or the truth about the 'man of lawlessness' being a counterfeit? When we consider this whole issue we have, in essence, the following sequence:

1) The lie — Lawlessness (the separation from Torah) working secretly today. The result of false teaching (Christianity).
2) The truth — The exposure of the lie (This book).
3) Acceptance of the truth by the wise, that is, those whose names are written in the book of life.
4) Rejection of the truth by the unwise.
5) Elohim's delusion — the counterfeit messiah promoting the lie (Christianity).
6) The acceptance of the delusion by the unwise. That is those who are not wise enough to accept the truth. These are the ones whose names are not written in the Book of Life, the ones who will be amazed by the power of the counterfeit and follow him, the act of 'falling away.'
7) The Day of YHWH — Elohim's wrath.

From the above sequence of events, the truth cannot be associated with the exposure of the counterfeit because the counterfeit is YHWH's subsequent punishment for those who do not accept the truth. Therefore we have to be referring to the exposure of the Christian faith for what it truly is. First the truth is made known and the deceitful nature of Christianity revealed. Those whose names are written in the Book of Life will accept the truth, all others will reject it thereby entering into rebellion against YHWH and 'falling away.' Those that fall away will be deluded by the counterfeit messiah, as intended by YHWH and readily follow him continuing with their Christian worship. By leading the world to Christianity *after* its exposure as a false religion, the counterfeit is exposed for what he truly is, the man of lawlessness, as confirmed in the latter part of verse 3. When the 'falling away' is complete that is, all those whose names are not written in the Book of Life are following the counterfeit messiah, YHWH's wrath, (the Day of YHWH) will happen. This is the particular event that ends the dominion of the four beasts described as ruling for 'a season and a time.' in Daniel chapter 7 and discussed in Part 1.

With its publication this book will categorize mankind into those who accept the truth and those who do not.

> My people are destroyed for want of knowledge. (HOSEA 4:6)

Whilst a lack of knowledge is the same as ignorance and ignorance can be quite innocent, when the truth is learnt and rejected, ignorance then becomes rebellion. It is to this state of rebellion against YHWH's truth that the phrase, 'falling away' refers. It is falling away from the truth, from righteousness, from YHWH Himself.

Let us now consider the final verse remaining of 2 Thessalonians, verse 8b:

> VERSE 8B : whom the Master shall consume with the Spirit of His mouth and bring to naught with the manifestation of His coming.

The counterfeit will succeed in all he wishes; after all he is Elohim's delusion and has Elohim's support in all he does. Nobody will be capable of opposing him. Only Yeshua's return will bring his reign on earth to an end. YHWH will allow this situation to continue only until the 'falling away' is complete. Then YHWH's wrath will commence and Messiah will return but only YHWH knows when that will be. Not even Messiah Yeshua is aware; referring to His return Messiah Yeshua tells His disciples:

> "But when that day and hour will come, no one knows – not the angels in heaven not the Son, only the Father." (MATTHEW 24:36)

It is comforting to know that YHWH is at all times in total control of all things. Even Satan and all his demons are under the authority of the one Creator of the universe, YHWH:

> ... because in connection with Him were created all things – in heaven and on earth, visible and invisible, whether thrones or lordships, rulers or authorities – they have been created through him and for Him. (COLOSSIANS 1:16)

'All things were created for Him,' as we have just said the whole of creation is YHWH's armoury.

MORE ON THE NUMBER 666

At this point we need to finish our examination of the number of the beast: 666.

> Also it forces everyone – great and small, rich and poor, free and slave – to receive a mark on his right hand or on his forehead preventing anyone from buying or selling unless he has the mark, that is, the name of the beast or the number of its name. This is where wisdom is needed; those who understand should count the number of the beast, for it is the number of a person, and its number is 666. (REVELATION 13:16–18)

We discussed in Part 1 how the number 666 is both a name and a title. How it applies to the Pope via the Vatican labelling Popes 'Vicar of Jesus Christ' and how the meaning behind this title is replacement of the son of god. But as there cannot be a replacement of the true Son of the true Elohim, the number/title/name designated 666 has to be that of a fake, a counterfeit. *This is the whole essence of this number or title; it is that of a fake.* Ironically, by affixing this title to the Pope the Vatican is confirming what the position/authority of Pope truly is — false. Through the Vatican, Elohim has revealed to us all the truth behind what this number means — counterfeit. It is the number of the beast from the pit and by the scriptures affixing this number to him we are forewarned that he is the fake messiah.

But why is YHWH revealing the very nature of His delusion prior to sending it? You would think it rather defeats the purpose of the delusion. The truth is YHWH does not want anyone to be deceived. He is the Elohim of truth, who claims 'all souls belong to Him' (Ezekiel 18:4), so why would he want to deceive that which he created? He doesn't. What YHWH wants is for all souls to return to Him. His delusion is not of His choosing but the result of mankind's rebellion against Him. We said previously that when the truth is known and rejected ignorance becomes rebellion. This is why the scriptures tell us that YHWH's delusion is only for those whose names are not written in the Book of Life. Those whose names are written in the Book of life are those with knowledge and understanding, as said in Revelation 13:8:

> ... those who understand should count the number of the beast, for it is the number of a person, and its number is 666.

Are you one with knowledge and understanding?

THE MARK OF THE BEAST

> Also it forces everyone – great and small, rich and poor, free and slave – to receive a mark on his right hand or on his forehead preventing anyone from buying or selling unless he has the mark, that is, the name of the beast or the number of its name. (REVELATION 13:16–17)

Verse 16 tells us that the second beast forces everyone to receive the mark of the beast on their right hand or forehead.

There has been much wild speculation about how this verse will be fulfilled. A common interpretation is that everyone will be physically marked in some way but with a proper understanding of the scriptures we should realise the nonsense of this. We have learnt that this number is that of the counterfeit messiah. Those who follow this counterfeit will be adopting for themselves a false belief and living a false life, by so doing they will be carrying the mark of the beast. To carry the mark of the beast is to follow that which is a fake. Insofar as the issue here is concerned it is to show allegiance to the beast power.

Consider the situation when you join a particular society or group. You are given the rules that all members are required to abide by. It is these rules that separate members from non members. Only by following the rules can members demonstrate their allegiance to that club or society. In effect the rules are the personal mark of that particular society or club. The mark of the beast is its system of religion. By following the beast's system of worship you are carrying its mark you are a member of the club.

Expanding further on this theme, almost all modern translations of Revelation 14:9 say, 'If anyone worships the beast and his image and receives his mark *on* his forehead or *on* his right hand.' The original King James Version of 1611, considered by scholars to be the most accurate translation says, 'If anyone worships the beast and his image and receives his mark *in* his forehead or *in* his hand.' In later revisions of the King James *in* was replaced with *on*, probably because the original wording was considered a printing error and not grammatically correct. Nevertheless, the original wording was very correct because the mark is your obedience and your obedience is *in* your mind. This fact is demonstrated by YHWH's own words, when in Jeremiah 31:33 YHWH says of His people Israel, that He will put His law in their minds. YHWH repeats his words in Hebrews 8:10 & 10:16: He will put His laws in their minds. YHWH's people are those who keep His commandments. In other words they are *'mindful'* of His commandments. They have a mind to obey Him. This is in contrast to those who have the mark of the beast and are mindful to follow the beast. But we are told not only is the mark in the forehead but also in the right hand. The term hand is commonly used to describe actions or acts: 'He did it by his own hand', or to describe ownership, 'he has been delivered out of the hand of Satan,' even to mark time, 'The Day of Elohim is at hand.' In these verses of Revelation its use is meant to describe the acts of people.

Obedience is *in* the mind, it's *in* the head hence the term, 'in the forehead.' But what of those who do not have a mind to obey, those who do not want to 'join the club.' Those who have no religious following and live unrighteous lives. These people qualify for the mark of the beast by their actions, that is, by the lifestyle they follow consequently, the mark is in their right hand.

But let us be very clear on an issue, the mark of the beast is *not* about transgression, it cannot be because we all transgress. The mark of the beast is about following a lifestyle that is outside YHWH's laws; outside His Torah. Remember the Torah (Genesis – Deuteronomy) is the only section of scripture containing all (not just the Ten Commandments) of YHWH's laws, given to Israel for the benefit of all humanity. Unless a person is living a lifestyle under the umbrella of Torah that person is following Satan.

Messiah Yeshua was referring to lifestyle when in Matthew 16:24 He said, "... take up his execution stake and keep following Me." This was an instruction to follow His Torah observant lifestyle. It is the person's lifestyle that YHWH is concerned with. Insofar as our transgressions are concerned, YHWH deals with these transgressions through His endless grace.

The inclusion of the term 'in their right hand' is of particular significance. Although the counterfeit will make everyone worship him or perish, this phrase tells us that not everyone will have a genuine desire to follow him. But in order to save their lives some will worship him physically, conforming in appearance only. Although these people will not have a heartfelt desire to follow the counterfeit, they will live a lifestyle conforming to his dictates. By so doing they will have his mark in their right hand.

THE MISNOMER OF 'ANTI CHRIST'

The term anti Christ has not been used in this book. This title makes no sense at all, because Christ is the messiah of a false religion. Satan supports and promotes all false religions so why would he be in opposition to its messiah. In order to give his deceit strength, Satan has created the illusion that he is against Christ and wants to destroy Christianity. In so doing he has given this false religion the appearance of truth. This is in fact Satan's own great delusion, a delusion that is being promoted by Christianity itself. Whilst under this delusion Christians have no chance of realising the truth of the scriptures. The truth is, Satan is not in opposition to Catholicism/Christianity anymore than he is in opposition to any of the other false religions, on the contrary, he's promoting them all. You cannot have a false religion with a true messiah. If this is the case then we will have to respect all religions.

SO WHO IS CHRISTIANITY'S JESUS?

So who is Christianity's Jesus? Well we know who he isn't. He isn't the Messiah who appeared on the earth 2000 years ago and is spoken of in YHWH's scriptures, that's certain:

- The Messiah who appeared 2000 years ago was not born in December.
- Scripture tells us that the messiah who appeared 2000 years ago, died and was resurrected at the time of the Pesach (Passover) Festival. Jesus on the other hand died and rose at Easter.
- The Messiah who appeared 2000 years ago instructed that not one yud or stroke (jot or tittle) of His Father's Torah (Law) will fade and He honoured all of His Father's festivals described in Leviticus 23. Whereas Jesus ended the law and His followers honour different festivals.
- Jesus Christ has to be a different messiah to the Jewish Messiah, Yeshua. Of the true Messiah, Yeshua, Luke 4:16 says:

> Now when he went to Natzeret (Nazareth), where He had been brought up, on Shabbat he went into the synagogue as usual. He stood up to read ...

This is a reference to the Saturday Shabbat, Sunday worship did not exist when Messiah Yeshua walked on the earth. YHWH did not decree two weekly Shabbats and His Son, Messiah Yeshua, observed all that His Father decreed. Those who worship on a Sunday must be following a different messiah to the one spoken of in YHWH's scriptures.

Clearly the Messiah who walked on earth 2000 years ago and Christianity's Jesus are not one and the same. They each were born, died and were resurrected at different times of the year. One kept His Father's Torah (Law), the other violated YHWH's Torah (Law). So if Jesus is not the one spoken of in the scriptures, just who is he? Obviously there cannot be two true Messiahs. The truth is he is a false messiah, the head of a false scriptures. It is this belief in a false messiah that the true Messiah, Yeshua, is referring to in Matthew 7:21–23:

> "Not everyone who says to me 'Master, Master' will enter the Kingdom of Heaven, only those who do what my Father in heaven wants. On that Day (Day of Judgement), many will say to me, 'Master, Master! Didn't we prophesy in your name? Didn't we expel demons in your name? Didn't we perform many miracles in your name?' Then I will tell them to their faces, 'I never knew you! Get away from me, you workers of lawlessness (Torahlessness).

There is enlightenment in these words of Messiah Yeshua that is generally not realised. He is forewarning of a counterfeit spiritual power that will manifest itself through miracle performing individuals. But Messiah Yeshua goes further and identifies these individuals. They are those who prophesy, exorcise demons and do wonders such as miraculous healing, believing their power is from Him. But their power is from a counterfeit source because Messiah Yeshua says, He never knew these people. Messiah Yeshua is not referring to Muslims, Buddhists or Hindus, Messiah Yeshua is talking of a counterfeit in 'His name' that is, a counterfeit who claims to be the Messiah of the scriptures, the Son of the Elohim of Israel. This excludes all other false religions except Christianity. Even Islamic belief is that god has no son, so Messiah Yeshua cannot be referring to Muslims. There is only one counterfeit that fits this description — Jesus Christ the messiah of Christianity. Only Christians prophesy, exorcise demons and heal, all in the name of the one who they believe is the Son of the Elohim of Israel but as confirmed by the words of the true Messiah himself, is an imposter. Messiah Yeshua's words are in effect a prophesy of Jesus Christ, the messiah of a lawless (Torahless) faith, a faith not based on the Father's instruction.

It is through these prophets, exorcists and healers that Satan's counterfeit spirit is alive and flourishing today. The efficacious results of these people is not questioned, they possess real powers. Unfortunately they are deceived into believing it to be holy power, whilst it is demonic. Revelation 16:14 confirms the presence of such a source of power and we are warned against such in Leviticus 19:31. By promoting Christ worship, these wondrous individuals, spoken of by Messiah Yeshua are serving Satan's cause and not YHWH's cause.

WHICH NAME — YESHUA OR JESUS

There are texts available alleging the name Jesus is the English translation of names originating from Greek mythology. It is claimed that Jesus is a derivative of the Greek name Iesous or Ieusus associated with the deity of healing allied to the kingdom of Zeus. If true, when we speak the name Jesus we are in reality accrediting the kingdom of Zeus because there is no difference between speaking the actual Greek name or a derivative of the name. What is more, it would mean using the name Jesus is a direct violation of YHWH's decree in Exodus:

> "Pay attention to everything I have said to you; do not invoke the names of other gods or even let them be heard crossing your lips." (EXODUS 23:13)

Notwithstanding the controversy surrounding this issue, prudence is to err on the side of caution. Are we prepared to risk being in violation of YHWH's decree? If we wait until judgment to learn the truth, we may find it is too late.

> It is time for leaders within the Messianic movement to accept that Christianity's Jesus is not our Messiah Yeshua by another name. Messiah Yeshua's words in Matthew 7:21 are an endorsement of this fact. Messiah Yeshua and Jesus are not one and the same and never will be. To interchange these names represents ignorance and leads one towards another messiah — a counterfeit Yeshua. Those who purport to be carrying the Messianic banner, yet use a counterfeit name for our Messiah or accept such usage by congregation members, need to wake up and shake off their ambivalence. By not correcting such an error they are failing in their role.

Using Messiah's correct name is important. YHWH set this principle in Exodus chapter 3 verses 13 and 15:

> VERSE 13 : Moshe (Moses) said to Elohim, "Look when I appear before the people of Israel and say to them, 'The Elohim of your ancestors has sent me to you,' and they ask me, 'What is his Name? What am I to tell them?'
>
> VERSE 15 : Elohim said further to Moshe, "Say this to the people of Israel: 'Yud-Heh-Vav-Heh (YHWH), the Elohim of your fathers, the Elohim of Avraham (Abraham), the Elohim of Yitz'chak (Isaac) and the Elohim of Ya'akov (Jacob), has sent me to you.'

YHWH goes on to proclaim:

> "This is My Name forever; this is how I am to be remembered generation after generation."

YHWH could not be more explicit in telling mankind how He is to be addressed. He is instructing His Name be used in all references to Him and there is a specific reason for Elohim giving this instruction. It is because other titles/names such as lord and god were commonplace and used in pagan worship. By using His Name we know the one we are addressing is the true Elohim of the universe. We know exactly to whom we are praying, who is the One listening and most importantly, who is the One answering our prayers. YHWH gave this instruction and set this principle for a reason. It is obviously important that He be correctly identified. It is clear that YHWH did not want to be confused with pagan gods. Referring to YHWH in such generic terms as god and lord is a direct violation of what He has instructed. Would He want it any different for the true Messiah, for His Son? Surely the same principle would apply to Messiah Yeshua. Whilst Messiah Yeshua did not proclaim His Name in the same way His Father did, He too would not want to be confused with false messiahs. To address Him using the name of the messiah of a religion not based on His Father's Torah (Law), is a violation of the principle set by YHWH in Exodus chapter 3. Substituting His correct name with Jesus is the true replacement theology and Messianic leaders have a responsibility to prevent this. Too often Messianic leaders are quite prepared to show flexibility so as not to 'rock the boat' or cause hurt. Let such leaders be reminded that Messiah Yeshua was executed, the

Prophets were killed and the Apostles tortured, all for the sake of the truth. Such indifference, where it exists, by the leadership needs to stop. The Messianic movement should not embrace Christian terminology in this way or any other way for that matter and needs to distance itself from all semblances of this apostate religion, as it does the others.

CONCLUSION TO PART 2

Some may have thought that the problem with Rome is wholly with the Papal custom it follows. After all it is this custom that separates the Catholic Church from the rest. But hopefully it has been shown that the end time apostasy is not confined to the Papal system itself. The scriptures number ten officials of the counterfeit; this does not correlate with the organisational structure of Rome or Catholicism. Therefore the phrase, 'image to the beast' used in Revelation 13:14 to describe the counterfeit's new administration, cannot be a reference to a system of administration modelled on the Vatican. Neither do the scriptures call the counterfeit a Pope, not even a 'little horn' but portray him as a counterfeit lamb (Revelation 13:11) and refer to him as the false prophet (Revelation 19:20). It is the principle of falsehood that is the connection between the counterfeit and Rome. We have seen how the number/title/name 666 is correctly given to the position of Pope, which having the label 'vicar of the son of god,' is itself the position of a counterfeit; a fake. It is for this reason the same number/title/name 666 is carried by the counterfeit messiah. But the apostasy described in the book of Revelation is not encompassed within the 666 issue, it is the other way around. The 666 falsehood is encompassed within the apostasy, that is, the apostasy is greater than the 666 falsehood itself.

Because the scriptures portray the counterfeit as a lamb, we know he comes masquerading as the true Messiah of the scriptures, Yeshua, and not as the head of another religion. When Messiah Yeshua returns He will administer His Father's Torah (Law) with an 'iron rod' that is, He will enforce YHWH's scriptures. In the case of the counterfeit, for his deception as the true Lamb of Elohim to succeed, he must be seen to fulfil prophesy. Because he is coming as the messiah spoken of in the scriptures, he also will invoke a form of worship that has a scriptural basis. But it is not the aim of the counterfeit to bring people back to YHWH. So he must invoke a deceitful system of worship. One that shrouds transgressions of YHWH's scriptures under the appearance of adherence to them. There already exists a scenario that fits this picture — Christianity, with its distortion of YHWH's scriptures. The seed of the end time apostasy is not in the Papal system of Rome but in the homogeneous religion promoted by Catholicism and the other church types. The truth is the apostasy has already been well received by 2 billion Christians, in preparation for their welcome reception of the counterfeit.

A BULLET FROM HEAVEN

PART THREE

PART THREE

Elohim's Truth

ELOHIM'S TRUTH

Because mankind has chosen to be unrighteous YHWH will provide a delusion for mankind. He has allowed mankind to follow a lie believing it to be the truth. In Parts 1 and 2 we revealed the lie that YHWH has allowed to be perpetuated throughout the world. So what is the truth? As stated at the beginning of Part 2 of this book, there can be only one truth: YHWH's truth, as contained in His Torah (Law) which He gave to the Israelite nation at Mount Sinai.

YHWH's Torah (Law) comprises the first five books of the scriptures, Breisheet (Genesis), Sh'mot (Exodus), Wayikra (Leviticus), Bamidbar (Numbers) and D'varim (Deuteronomy). It is here and only here that the Creator of the universe provides His directions for all mankind to follow. It is only in the Torah (Law) that you will find the route to righteousness.

This Part 3 deals with several common misconceptions with respect to Elohim's Torah (Law) and His plan for all humanity.

THE TORAH (LAW) WAS GIVEN TO ISRAEL?

YHWH intended for Israel to be different from the rest of mankind. The Israelite nation was to be a set apart (holy) nation. Israel was the only nation to have a specific relationship with the Creator of the universe. The foundation of this specific relationship is the covenant YHWH made with the Israelite nation through the patriarchs; Abraham, Isaac and Jacob. YHWH defines the covenant as:

> "... then I will be your Elohim and you will be My people." (JEREMIAH 7:23 & 11:4)

Just as with any covenant there are two parties: YHWH and the Israelite nation. Each party has rights and obligations. However, not until Israel arrived at Sinai, after leaving Egypt, did YHWH tell Israel what the rights and obligations pursuant to the covenant were to be. These rights and obligations are fully detailed throughout Exodus and Leviticus in the Torah (Law). Leviticus chapter 23 commences with YHWH telling Israel what He requires of them:

> YHWH said to Moshe (Moses), saying "Tell the people of Isra'el; 'The designated times of YHWH, which you are to proclaim as holy convocations are My designated times." (LEVITICUS 23:1)

From Leviticus 23 verse 2 and throughout whole of chapters 23, 24, 25, 26 and 27, YHWH then provides a comprehensive list of his rulings which the nation of Israel are to live by.

In Leviticus 26:3–12, YHWH tells the people how He will bless them if they keep His statutes *and* commandments:

> "If you live by my regulations, observe my mitzvot (commandments) and obey them; then I will provide the rain you need in its season, the land will yield its produce and the trees in the field will yield their fruit. Your threshing time will extend until the grape harvest and your grape harvesting will extend until the time for sowing seed. You will eat as much food as you want and live securely in your land.
>
> I will give shalom (peace) in the land – you will lie down to sleep unafraid of anyone. I will rid the land of wild animals. The sword will not go through your land. You will pursue your enemies, and they will fall before your sword. Five of you will chase a hundred, and a hundred of you will chase ten thousand – your enemies will fall before your sword.
>
> I will turn toward you, make you productive, increase your numbers and uphold My covenant with you. You will eat all you want from last years harvest and throw out what remains of the old to make room for the new. I will put My tabernacle among you, and I will not reject you, but I will walk among you and be your Elohim and you will be My people."

And in Deuteronomy 28:1–13:

> If you listen closely to what YHWH your Elohim says, observing and obeying all His mitzvot (commandments) which I am giving you today, YHWH your Elohim will raise you high above all the nations on earth, and all the following blessings will be yours in abundance – if you will do what YHWH your Elohim says;
>
> A blessing on you in the city and a blessing on you in the countryside.
>
> A blessing on the fruit of your body, the fruit of your land and the fruit of your livestock – the young of your cattle and flocks.
>
> A blessing on your grain basket and kneading bowl.
>
> A blessing on you when you go out and a blessing on you when you come in.
>
> YHWH will cause your enemies attacking you to be defeated before you; they will advance on you one way and flee before you seven ways.
>
> YHWH will order a blessing to be with you in your barns and in everything you undertake; He will bless you in the land YHWH your Elohim is giving you.
>
> YHWH will establish you as a people separated out for Himself, as He has sworn to you — if you observe the mitzvot of YHWH your Elohim and follow His ways. Then all the peoples on earth will see that YHWH's name, His presence, is with you; so that they will be afraid of you.
>
> YHWH will give you great abundance of good things — of the fruit of your body, the fruit of your livestock and the fruit of your land YHWH swore to your ancestors to give you. YHWH will open for you His good treasure, the sky, to give your land its rain at the right seasons and to bless everything you undertake. You will lend to many nations and not borrow
>
> YHWH will make you the head and not the tail; and you will be only above and not below.

Even before YHWH confirmed the above blessings He gave Israel an exceptional promise, declared in Exodus 23:25–26:

> 'You are to observe YHWH your Elohim; and He will bless your food and water. I will take sickness away from among you. In your land your women will not miscarry or be barren, and you will live out the full span of your lives.

What a tremendous assurance from the above passages, a guarantee of success in all you do and not to suffer any sickness or illness as long as you live. Can you imagine such an existence?

In essence the covenant relationship can be illustrated as follows:

PARTIES TO THE COVENANT	RIGHTS	OBLIGATIONS
Israelite Nation	To receive the blessings detailed in the Torah (Law)	To live a Torah observant lifestyle
YHWH	For Israel to observe His Torah(Law)	To bless and protect the nation of Israel

This was the basis of the covenant relationship.

THE PURPOSE OF ELOHIM'S COVENANT RELATIONSHIP WITH ISRAEL

Have you ever wondered why YHWH, who created all mankind, would choose a particular people for Himself? After all He tells us in Ezekiel 18:4 that all souls belong to Him and in John 3:16 we are told that YHWH so loved the world, (not just Israel) that He gave His only begotten Son. This being so, how could the one who Created us all chose one people to be His own at the exclusion of everyone else?

The truth is, YHWH's covenant with Israel was never intended to be at the exclusion of the rest of mankind. Quite the reverse, YHWH's covenant relationship with Israel was for the benefit of all mankind. YHWH needed a mechanism by which all mankind would be drawn back to Him and to establish a covenant relationship with a particular nation was the mechanism He chose. YHWH's covenant relationship with Israel was to be the example for all mankind to follow. Through His covenant relationship with Israel, YHWH intended for all mankind to establish a Torah (Law) based relationship with

Him. By their special relationship Israel was to be the light leading all mankind to Him:

> "I YHWH called you righteously, I took hold of you by the hand. I shaped you and made you a covenant for the people, to be a light for the Goyim (Gentiles)." (ISAIAH 42:6)

> "For just as a loincloth clings to a man's body, I made the whole house of Israel and the whole house of Y'hudah (Judah) cling to Me, says YHWH, so that they could be My people, building Me a name and becoming for Me a source of praise and honour." (JEREMIAH 13:11)

YHWH intended for Israel's reward; His blessings over them, to be so great they would be the envy of all nations. Other nations would loose faith in their own gods and seek the Elohim of Israel, the one true Elohim. The Gentiles too, would want this blessed lifestyle. This is what is meant by the phrase, 'for Me a source of praise and honour' in Jeremiah. This was how Israel was to be a light to the Gentiles.

THE LEVEL OF COMMITMENT THE TORAH (LAW) REQUIRES OF ISRAEL

Contained in verses 1–17 of Exodus chapter 20 are the Ten Commandments and many believe that these constitute the total commitment required by the Torah (Law). But these are only the beginning. Throughout the remaining chapters of Exodus and in Leviticus, YHWH provides a whole compendium of additional rulings, precepts etc. After which, He confirms His requirement for the nation of Israel to observe all (not just the Ten Commandments) that He has given:

> "But if you will not listen to Me and obey all these mitzvot (commandments), if you loathe My regulations and reject My rulings, in order not to obey all My mitzvot but cancel My covenant; then I, for My part, will do this to you; ..." (LEVITICUS 26:14)

Even before the Sinai experience, YHWH indicates that what is required is full observance of all His rulings, statutes etc:

> A famine came over the land, not the same as the first famine, which had taken place when Avraham (Abraham) was

> alive . Yitz'chak (Isaac) went to G'rar to Avimelekh king of the P'lishtim. YHWH appeared to him and said "Don't go down to Egypt, but live where I tell you. Stay in this land and I will be with you and bless you, because I will give all these lands to you and to your descendants. I will fulfil the oath which I swore Avraham your father – I will make your descendants as numerous as the stars in the sky, I will give all these lands to your descendants and by your descendants all the nations of the earth will bless themselves. All this is because Avraham heeded what I said and did what I told him to do – he followed my mitzvot (commandments), my regulations and my teachings." (GENESIS 26:1–5)

Abraham was blessed not because he kept YHWH's commandments alone but kept the whole of the Torah (Law).

Psalm 119:1–7 further expands the theme of obedience by defining what is required for a person to be considered righteous in YHWH's eyes:

> How happy are those whose way of life is blameless, who live by the Torah (Law) of YHWH! How happy are those who observe His instruction, who seek Him wholeheartedly! They do nothing wrong but live by His ways. You laid down your precepts for us to observe with care. May my ways be steady in observing your statutes. Then I will not be put to shame, since I will have fixed my sight on all your mitzvot (commandments).

In this Psalm the word Torah (Law) is repeated 25 times, instruction (testimonies) is repeated 22 times, way being the pattern of life dictated by Elohim's Torah (Law) occurs 11 times, precepts 21 times, statutes 21 times, commandments 22 times, rulings (judgments) can be found 23 times.

The nation of Israel has never been under any misconceptions of what the Torah (Law) requires of them. The issue of commitment is a problem within Christianity, not Judaism or the Messianic community. Unfortunately, Christianity promotes a theology advocating that the Torah (Law) was meant for Israel and is of less effect for those not of Jewish descent. Several of the salient points forming this unscriptural theology are now examined in the following section.

THE TRUE RELEVANCE OF TORAH (LAW) FOR CHRISTIANS

A) THE MISNOMER OF THE TERM LAW

It was stated in the Introduction to this book that the Hebrew 'torah' does not mean 'law'. To accurately define a Hebrew word it is necessary to establish the root from which the word itself is derived. The word torah comes from the root 'horah', causative verb 'yarah', which means to teach, instruct or guide. Contrary to common perception, the root does not convey the concept of a legalistic list of do's and don'ts but rather, 'to aim at,' to point to. Whilst the Torah does comprise several legal elements, being: mitzvot, chukim and mishpatim; commandments, ordinances and judgements in English; these must be understood in terms of the true concept embodied within the Torah itself. An analogy may be to compare the Torah with a suit of armour. The suit of armour protects its contents from external forces, in other words it is a means of preservation, protecting what is inside from possible degradation from the outside. This is very much the true concept of the Torah (Law); to protect/preserve those who are under its umbrella from the corruption of the outside world. It is YHWH's means of providing a safe environment for His people, thereby preserving them until the time allotted for their salvation. When the Torah is understood in these terms, the translators could not find an equivalent in the Greek language which accurately conveyed such a concept embodied within a legal framework. The translators decided on the Greek word 'nomos' which means to 'parcel', with secondary meanings of law or regulation. Unfortunately the law definition has been adopted in English translations with regrettable consequences. The Torah (Law) is not an antiquated list of law irrelevant to the believers of today, as is often preached on a Sunday. It is the only means of protection, a personal suit of armour provided by YHWH Himself for all who wish wear it. But to be effective the whole of the armour must be worn. If a piece is missing the protection is flawed.

Having now established the true meaning of the Hebrew 'torah' not to mean 'law' but teaching or instruction, for the following section (B), the usual suffix (Law) has been replaced with the more accurate suffix (YHWH's instruction), in an effort to remove the illegitimate concept propagated with the usage of the term law.

B) CHRISTIANS ARE NOT UNDER THE TORAH (YHWH'S INSTRUCTION)

A frequent statement coming from the mouths of Christians is, "We are not under the Law," in effect not under the Torah, not under YHWH's instruction. On occasion some will further amplify this statement continuing, "We are under grace." Consider the following from the epistle of John:

> 'Everyone who keeps sinning is violating Torah (YHWH's instruction) – indeed sin is a violation of Torah (YHWH's instruction). (1 JOHN 3:4)

What could be plainer; here we have the scriptural definition of sin: it is a transgression against Torah that is, a transgression against the instructions YHWH has stipulated mankind should follow. According to this scripture it is impossible for a person to transgress if they are not under YHWH's instruction; His Torah. All of us, Christians and non Christians alike, are cable of transgression, therefore, in terms of the above scripture, all of us are subject to the Torah. The real contention is, how much of the Torah is applicable to non-Jewish people. Ironically, even those Christians who claim not to be under the Torah, will readily concede that they are subject to the Ten Commandments, which of course are embodied within the Torah. The cause of this apparent oxymoron is, as was intimated earlier, the Christian theology advocating a significant abandonment of the Torah, of YHWH's instruction, for all Christians

It is impossible to align any theology encouraging a 'shrinking of the Torah,' with either the prophetic picture painted by the Tanakh (Old Testament), with the words of Messiah Himself or with what is said by the Apostles.. Indeed, any teaching promoting so much as the slightest negation of YHWH's Torah (instruction), stands in blatant defiance of what is decreed by the Father:

> 'Do not add to what I am giving you and do not subtract from it.' (DEUTERONOMY 4:2)

What is decreed by the Son, Messiah Yeshua:

> "Don't think I have come to abolish the Torah (YHWH's instruction) or the Prophets, I have not come to abolish but to complete." (MATTHEW 5:17)
>
> 'Yes indeed! I tell you that until heaven and earth pass away, not so much as a yud or stroke will pass away from the Torah (YHWH's instruction) – not until everything that must happen has happened." (MATTHEW 5:18)

What is decreed by the apostle Paul:

> 'For it is not merely the hearers of the Torah (YHWH's instruction) whom Elohim considers righteous; rather, it is the doers of what Torah (YHWH's instruction) says who will be made righteous in Elohim's sight.' (ROMANS 2:13)

Each of the quotations above is absolute; definitive. The Apostle's words tell us that the Father's instruction is, of course, applicable to all including Gentiles. Note, in both instances Paul uses the definite article. He does not say 'some of' or 'a portion of,' he says, 'the Torah'. Paul's words show perfect correlation with Messiah Yeshua's clarification in Matthew 5:18, that all of the Father's instruction is applicable, every single command down to the last word.

Possibly the most profound statement concerning observance of YHWH's Torah, His instruction, is found in Proverbs 28:9:

> If a person will not listen to Torah (YHWH's instruction) even his prayer is an abomination.

This proverb is astounding, for those who neglect to observe YHWH's instruction, which according to the decrees above, can only mean full observance of all He has given, praying is not only a waste of time, it is an abomination.

The decrees stated above are taken from the front of the scriptures – Deuteronomy, the middle of the scriptures – Proverbs and the end of the scriptures – New Testament; evidence that Torah compliance is a continuous theme throughout the whole of the scriptures: starting with Moses, followed by the Prophets, then Messiah Yeshua and finally by the Apostles themselves. Yet Christians are led to believe:

1) The Messiah brought an end to the Torah (YHWH's instruction).
2) Christians are under grace not Torah (YHWH's instruction).
3) The section containing the Ten Commandments is the only portion of the Torah (YHWH's instruction) that is applicable to Christians.

This apostate teaching has been so convincingly cloaked with authenticity; it is accepted by two billion Christians as bona-fide. Although all of the above arguments are integral, the fundamentals behind each argument are tangential, so for simplicity each argument is considered individually. Items 2 and 3 are dealt with in the following sections. Here we will consider item 1 above and examine some words from Paul that are offered in support of the annulment of YHWH's Torah: His instruction. A good example is Romans 10:4 which in most bibles is rendered:

> 'For Messiah is the end of the law for righteousness to everyone who believes.'

Such a presentation is very disappointing; inferring if one believes in Messiah there is no longer any need to obey YHWH's Torah (instruction). Such a hypothesis is, as it sounds, ridiculous. This misconception is the result of a poor effort in translating from the Greek. If only those translating had paid more attention to what is said elsewhere in the scriptures: particularly where Paul himself advocates obedience to YHWH's Torah. Scripture is never contradictory! If it was we would all be lost, not knowing what to believe. Contradiction is generally the result of one or more of the following errors:

- a wrong or weak translation.
- a failure to consider other verses elsewhere in the scriptures and impacting on the topic.

- A lack of contextual recognition — a failure to correctly identify the subject concerning the scriptural passage under consideration.

It would require an acrobatic mind of some ability to find any harmony between Romans 10:4 as presented above and the decrees of the Father, Messiah Yeshua and the Apostle Paul himself, listed earlier.

As said, the problem here is in the English translation of the Greek. The English word 'end' is a translation of the Greek 'telos.' But the Greek 'telos' has several meanings depending on the context of its usage: 'telos' can mean termination, the aim, goal or purpose of. It can even have the meaning of tax. It is therefore important to establish the correct usage. For this it is necessary, 1) to accurately identify the subject issue of the surrounding verses and 2) the interpretation must always avoid contention with other scriptures. The above wording of Romans 10:4 certainly conflicts with Messiah Yeshua's words in Matthew 5:18.

In Matthew 5:17 Messiah Yeshua says He has not come to destroy or annul the Torah (YHWH's instruction) but to complete, some translations say fulfil, the Torah. When we take into account Messiah Yeshua's declaration, a more suitable and perfectly legitimate translation of the Greek 'telos' is goal or aim. In other words Messiah is the aim or the goal of the Torah; of YHWH's instruction. This same verse in the Complete Jewish Bible, the translation we are using, reads:

> For the goal at which the Torah aims is the Messiah, who offers righteousness to everyone who trusts.

What a difference. Far from creating controversy or confusion the verse now correlates with the rest of the scriptures and what we have said in Annexure 1 to Part 1 of this book. A part of Stern's commentary on this verse is worth repeating here:

> "The goal at which the Torah aims is acknowledging and trusting in the Messiah who offers, on the ground of this trusting, the very righteousness they are seeking."

The purpose of the Torah (YHWH's instruction) is to point towards salvation; to Messiah Yeshua and here is the endorsement: you cannot be of Messiah Yeshua and not of Torah. That would be the same as taking the Torah out of Messiah Yeshua, which is impossible.

If the nub of this particular Church theology is that a person cannot be saved by the Torah (YHWH's instruction) but only by grace, there can be no argument. The question is what has changed? The Torah was never a means of redemption. Rather, the Torah is meant for those already redeemed in YHWH's sight. In other words, a redeemed person will have a Spirit led desire to obey the lifestyle prescribed in the Torah, that is, in full obedience to His instructions. Christians need to recognise that what is prescribed is a complete lifestyle, given not just for Israel alone but for them to be the example for the whole of humanity to follow. In being selective with what YHWH has provided the Church has put itself above the Elohim it alleges to worship. From where does the Church get authority to treat YHWH's Torah as cannon fodder for human discretion? Nowhere in the scriptures is such authority bestowed upon humanity. When we do interfere, life becomes confused, out of focus. The consequence of a selective approach to the Torah is evident today via the confusion within the Church, with Christianity adopting both Saturday and Sunday worship whilst at the same time, agreeing only one day of the week has been sanctified and made holy.

C) TORAH (LAW) VERSES GRACE

Another unscriptural theology embodied within Christianity is that believers are under grace at the expense of the Torah (Law). The Church teaching that, with the advent of Messiah's atonement mankind is no longer under the Torah (Law) but under grace, infers that if you are under grace you are not under the Torah (Law). If this was meant to be the case, then why did YHWH say that His commandments, rulings, ways, precepts, statutes etc were to be kept generation after generation, without any limitation? Was YHWH forgetting about grace?

It should be realised that grace has existed since the time of creation itself and probably before, if we consider that Lucifer and those who followed him have, only by YHWH's grace, been allowed to live. It was by YHWH's grace that Adam and Eve were allowed to live after sinning against Him. From the following examples it can be seen that YHWH's grace was not introduced to mankind through the death and resurrection of Messiah Yeshua but existed long before:

> 'But Noah found grace in the sight of Elohim.' (GENESIS 6:8)

The words of Lot to YHWH's messengers in Genesis 19:19:

> 'Look please your servant has found favour in your eyes.'

It was by YHWH's grace that Israel's slavery under Pharaoh was brought to an end.

If YHWH's grace can be found in the first book of the scriptures, do you not think it will be present throughout the scriptures? Indeed, you will find examples of YHWH's grace in almost every book of scripture from the first to the last. Undoubtedly grace and Torah (Law) have coexisted for millennia, one cannot replace the other because they are different. One is not a substitute for the other, on the contrary, the one is complementary to the other, and that is, Torah (Law) complements grace.

The foundation of this unscriptural theology is twofold. On the one hand, it is the result of a gross misinterpretation of the epistles of Paul, particularly Romans and Galatians, which we will deal with in a moment. On the other hand, it stems from a very virulent anti Jewish rhetoric by the church fathers of old. This anti Jewish rhetoric encompassed not only the Jewish people but also their culture, particularly their devout adherence to the Torah (Law). One of the roots of such anti-Semitic teaching is the accusation that the Jews are all Christ killers and their culture, including their Torah (Law) has no place in the Church. John Chrysostom a fifth century monk and acknowledged in most bible colleges as one of the prominent church fathers, wrote the following about the Jewish people and their culture:

> 'He who can never love Christ enough will never have done fighting against them (the Jews) who hate him. Flee then their assemblies, flee their houses and far from venerating the synagogue, because of the books it contains, hold it in hatred and aversion. I hate the synagogue precisely because it has the law and the prophets.'

Another quotation of similar vein is that from the Protestant reformer Martin Luther from the sixteenth century:

> 'Their synagogues should be set on fire ... Their homes should likewise be broken down and destroyed ... They should be deprived of their prayer books and talmuds ... Their Rabbis must be forbidden, under threat of death, to teach anymore ... Passport and traveling privileges should be absolutely forbidden ... Let the young and strong Jews and Jewesses be given the flail, the axe, the hoe, the spade, the distaff and the spindle and let them earn their bread by the sweat of their noses'

These and other similar condemnations of the Jewish people have all been used by the Church to discourage believers from following Jewish ways and distance themselves from YHWH's Torah (Law). Ariel & D'vorah Berkowitz in their book 'Torah Rediscovered' summarize the situation wonderfully with their comment:

> 'After centuries of anti-Jewish, anti Torah, and even anti-Semitic teaching from the most influential leaders of the Church, no one (in the church) would dare attempt to follow one of its (Torah's) precepts or teach others to do so.' Parenthesis added.

The other basis upon which this unscriptural theology is rooted, is the gross misinterpretation of what Paul has written in Romans and Galatians. It has to be said that a superficial reading of some of the phrases used by Paul would indeed lead a person to conclude that Paul is against YHWH's Torah (Law). But to interpret Paul as being against YHWH's Torah (Law) makes no sense when we consider what is said in Acts 21:20–24 and 24:14. Here we are told that Paul *lived a Torah (Law) observant life* and encouraged others to do the same. Paul was not a hypocrite, so we cannot therefore interpret his writings as anti Torah (Law). Instead, we must interpret his letters in a context agreeing with what is said in Acts and the lifestyle he lived. Let us now consider some of the phrases used by the Church to discourage believers from observance of YHWH's Torah (Law):

Romans 6:14:

> "For sin shall not have dominion over you for you are not under law but under grace." (NKJV)

Galatians 5:18:

> "But if you are led by the Spirit you are not under the law." (NKJV)

Ephesians 2:8–9:

> "For by grace are you saved through faith; and that not of yourselves, it is the gift of Elohim, not of works, lest anyone should boast." (NKJV)

Prima Facie there appears no argument, Paul's statements are quite clear the law is not applicable and we must live by grace. However, when we stop and take time to consider the context of these verses we then realise, the issue Paul is dealing with is that of salvation. The above verses were meant to allay the belief that a person could maintain the salvation they had received by grace, by their obedience to the Torah (Law). It is this premise of 'justification by works' that Paul is condemning, not the relevance of YHWH's Torah (Law) to the believer. Paul knew that the Torah (Law) was never intended by YHWH to be a means of salvation. Salvation can only be achieved through faith in Messiah Yeshua and received by the grace of YHWH Himself. Nonetheless, YHWH's grace is not offered at the expense of His Torah (Law). Such a misconception can only gain credence at the exclusion of what Paul says elsewhere:

> 'Therefore we conclude that a man is justified by faith apart from the deeds of the Torah (Law). (ROMANS 3:28) (NKJV)

In this passage Paul is explaining that justification is something separate from (apart from) the Torah. He then continues, telling the congregation that far from annulling the Torah (Law) faith confirms it:

> 'Do we then make void the Torah (Law) through faith? Certainly not, on the contrary we establish the Torah (Law). (ROMANS 3:31) (NKJV)

To this passage we can add Messiah Yeshua's comment:

> "... not so much as a yud or a stroke will pass from the Torah (Law) — not until everything that must happen has happened." (MATTHEW 5:18)

We are saved by YHWH's grace which He extends to us through our faith (belief) in His Son, Messiah Yeshua. However, if we are to live a new life in Messiah Yeshua, then YHWH's Torah (Law) will indeed be on our hearts, thereby fulfilling that what is said in Romans 3:31. Messiah's words above show that we cannot be of Messiah and not of YHWH's Torah (Law). Christianity needs to extinguish the belief that 'being saved' is an end in and of itself and should recognise that salvation on its own does little other than prepare a person for a Torah (Law) observant life. Once again Ariel & D'vorah Berkowitz in their book 'Torah Rediscovered' tell it well:

> 'The Torah describes what our changed life is to be. It does not cause our changed life. That is the miraculous work of Elohim, born of His grace.'

As was explained above the Hebrew word 'torah' does not mean law it means instruction. Are we then at liberty to say we are no longer under YHWH's instruction? Paul would never advocate ignoring YHWH's instruction. How could he, when in 2 Timothy 3:16 he says:

> "*All* scripture is Elohim breathed and is valuable for teaching the truth, convicting of sin, correcting faults and training in right living; thus anyone who belongs to Elohim may be fully equipped for every good work."

Remember there was no New Testament when Paul spoke these words, he was referring to the Tanakh (Old Testament), that is, the Torah, the Prophets and the Writings.

D) ONLY THE TEN COMMANDMENTS ARE APPLICABLE TODAY?

Within His Torah (Law) YHWH has provided a total of 613 rulings. But Christianity teaches the only portion of YHWH's Torah (Law) that is applicable to believers today, is that containing the Ten Commandments. The effect of this teaching is to redefine the meaning of Torah (Law) for New Testament purposes, thereby creating a new Torah (Law), albeit an extraction of the Old Testament Torah (Law). Such a philosophy not only destroys the intricacy between the two testaments, it annuls the prophetic picture of the Messiah as portrayed in the Torah (Law) and yet to be fulfilled.

The crux of this erroneous teaching is that only the Ten Commandments were written by Elohim. It is alleged that all of the other rulings were not only written by Moses but were also his creation and therefore they do not apply outside the nation of Israel. Such teaching can only come from the mouths of those who are either ignorant of what the scriptures say or prefer to ignore what the scriptures say. Firstly, in verse 22 of Exodus chapter 20, it is YHWH who is instructing Moses what regulations the people are to obey. The following chapters, 21 through 23, describe a very protracted list describing the lifestyle His people are to adopt: but it is clear at the beginning of this list who is dictating the information. In the first verse of chapter 21 it says:

> "These are the rulings you are to present to them."

It is clear who is speaking, the 'you' refers to Moses and the 'them' refers to the people. Now consider the content in Exodus 24:1–3:

> To Moshe(Moses) YHWH said, "Come up to YHWH – you Aharon, Nadav, Avihu and seventy of the leaders of Israel. Prostrate yourselves at a distance, whilst Moshe alone approaches YHWH – the others are not to approach and the people are not to go up with him." *Moshe came and told the people everything YHWH had said, including all the rulings.* The people answered with one voice. "We will obey every word YHWH has spoken."

A great deal more law is given in Leviticus chapters 23 through 27. Each chapter commences with the same words: YHWH said to Moses,

> "Tell the people of Israel ..."

The scriptures show clearly that all was given by YHWH to Moses for him to record and present to the nation. Of course all was written by Moses, he was Elohim's conduit to the people.

Let us now consider a different arrow but from the same quiver. The argument that all the additional rulings written in Moses' hand have become obsolete with Messiah's sacrifice. Colossians 2:14 is the strength submitted for this hypothesis:

> "Having wiped out the handwriting of requirements that was against us, which was contrary to us. And He has taken it out of the way, having nailed it to the cross." (COLOSSIANS 2:14) (NKJV)

Building on the premise that only the Ten Commandments were written by Elohim and all the other rulings were from Moses himself, it is offered by church leaders that the phrase, 'handwriting of requirements' refers to the writings of Moses and that it is these writings that have been 'nailed to the stake (cross).'

In Part 1 it was explained how the annual festivals given in Leviticus are YHWH's cycles referred to in Psalm 23. *These cycles are the only route to righteousness there is no other route.* Nevertheless these cycles, essential as they are, are not contained within the Ten Commandments. Therefore they are, according to the above philosophy, the handwriting of Moses and are no longer of any effect having been nailed to the stake with Messiah Yeshua. Yet the opening verse of Acts chapter 2, tells us that the disciples were gathered together to celebrate the Festival of Shavuot (Pentecost) when they received the Ruach HaKodesh (HS). Also Acts chapter 20 verse 16 says that the Apostle Paul was in a hurry to leave Asia Minor, being desirous to be in Jerusalem to celebrate the Festival of Shavuot. Later in his first epistle chapter 5 verses 7–8, we learn of Paul encouraging the Corinthian congregation to honour the Pesach (Passover) festival in the correct manner. Didn't the Apostles realise that these regulations had earlier been made obsolete having been, 'nailed to the stake?'

Continuing this theme, consider the four preliminary rules the Jewish elders and Paul imposed on the Gentile believers, explained in Acts 15. These four rulings are from that part of the Torah (Law) outside the Ten Commandments which again, according to Church philosophy, had also previously been made obsolete. In his last chapter Zechariah, when prophetically referring to the Day of YHWH and apparently the subsequent Millennial rule of Messiah, he informs his readers that those who are remaining will, as decreed by YHWH, travel to Jerusalem to celebrate the Festival of Sukkot (Tabernacles). It takes little effort to reveal the unscriptural dispensational theology being preached today, a philosophy that is fuelling apostasy.

It was further explained in Annexure 1 to Part 1 how YHWH's festivals are a prophetic picture of Messiah Yeshua himself. With His first coming, death and resurrection, He has fulfilled (not annulled) only part of this prophetic picture. What remains are the latter festivals which are prophetic of His second coming. To assert that Messiah's death brought a premature end to this prophetic picture (nailing the festivals to the stake) is in essence, to deny a second coming. Yet all Christianity awaits this very event.

We need now to take a closer look at Paul's narrative in Acts 15:

> "Therefore, my opinion is that we should not put obstacles in the way of the Goyim (Gentiles) who are turning to Elohim. Instead, we should write them a letter telling them to abstain from things polluted by idols, from fornication, from what is strangled and from blood." (ACTS 15:19–20)
>
> For from the earliest times, Moshe (Moses) has had in every city those who proclaim him, with his words being read in the synagogues every Shabbat (Sabbath)." (ACTS 15:21)

Acts 15:19–20 are the verses often presented as justification for the argument that non-Jewish believers are not subject to the whole of YHWH's Torah (Law) but are under a 'diluted' Torah (Law). But such an interpretation takes no cognizance of what is said in verse 21. This verse has to be understood in terms of the encouragement the elders were offering the Gentile believers, advocating their continued growth in the Torah. For this, they needed to listen to the Torah teachers preaching the 'Books of Moses' — the Torah (Law) every Shabbat, in the synagogue. Indeed the former verses are not an attempt to reduce the applicability of YHWH's Torah (Law) to Gentile believers but more accurately demonstrate the compassion and patience the elders had for the Torah-illiterate Gentile believers. Unlike their Jewish counterparts, for many Gentile believers the Torah was strange and the Jewish elders knew it was inappropriate to expect Gentile believers to follow the Torah with the same passion as did the Jewish people. Instead the elders stipulated the initial minimum requirement that would be necessary for the Gentiles to be welcomed in the synagogues by their Jewish counterparts. However, the elders not only expected but required the Gentile believers to attend the synagogue every Shabbat for continued learning and growth in the whole Torah (Law). Understand that it would be the whole Torah (Law) that would be preached in the synagogue, not just the Ten Commandments.

E) THE ORAL LAW – PAUL'S REAL PROBLEM IN ROMANS AND GALATIANS

Another issue that Paul had to deal with that is not so well known in Christian circles was the oral Torah. Christians may not appreciate that there are two Torahs, two laws. One is the Torah (Law) given by Elohim to Israel at Sinai, referred to as the written Torah or written Law. The other is the Pharisaic or rabbinical law known as the oral torah, oral law or Talmud (Hebrew). The Pharisees, Sadducees and scribes who were the religious leaders in Paul's day were the forerunners of today's Rabbis and the oral law is today referred to as rabbinical law. This rabbinical law is the law the religious leaders themselves imposed upon the Jewish people. The religious leaders felt that embellishment of the written Torah was necessary for it to become a 'workable' document. Whilst there are parts of the Talmud that provide helpful clarifications and insight with respect to complying with the requisites of the written Torah, the Talmud also contains sections that go beyond it's 'helpful status', introducing its own rules and making obedience to the written Torah needlessly burdensome. It was these unhelpful embellishments of His Torah (Law) that YHWH condemned in Jeremiah:

> "How can you say 'We are wise, YHWH's Torah is with us,' when in fact the lying pen of the scribes has turned it into falsehood." (JEREMIAH 8:8)

Similarly it is these sections of the oral torah, not the written Torah of YHWH, that Paul speaks against in his epistles and which Messiah Yeshua was continually condemning. A good example is the rebuke by Messiah Yeshua to the Pharisees when they complained that His disciples did not wash their hands before eating. Such washing is not mentioned in the written Torah (Law) of Elohim but was one of the laws imposed by the religious leaders themselves. Matthew 15:1–9:

> Then some P'rushim (Pharisees) and Torah (Law) teachers from Yerushalayim (Jerusalem) came to Yeshua and asked Him, "Why is it that your talmidim (disciples) break the Tradition of the Elders? (The man made rules of the religious leaders). They don't do n'tilat-yadayim (wash their hands) before they eat."
>
> He answered, "Indeed, why do you break the commandment of Elohim by your tradition? *For Elohim said* 'Honour your father and mother and anyone who curses his father or mother must be put to death.'
>
> *But you say,* 'If anyone says to his father or mother 'I have promised to give to Elohim what I might have used to help you — then his is rid of his duty to honour his father or mother. Thus by your tradition you make null and void the word of Elohim.' You hypocrites! Yesha'yahu (Isaiah) was right when he prophesied about you;
>
> These people honour Me with their lips but their hearts are far away from Me. Their worship of Me is useless, because they teach *manmade rules as if they were doctrines.*"

Messiah Yeshua said He has not come to abolish the Torah (Law) (Matthew 5:17), of course He was referring to the written Torah of

His Father. This being true, what authority has Paul to abolish it and why would he denounce the very rules by which he lived? We must interpret Paul's letters in the knowledge that he was a devout follower of YHWH's, written Torah (Law). To conclude, how could the Apostles advocate the obsolescence of YHWH's Torah (Law) when in the book of James, it is referred to as the 'Perfect Torah' and the 'Royal Torah: James 1:25 and 2:8 respectively.

F) THE LEVEL OF COMMITMENT THE TORAH (LAW) REQUIRES OF GENTILE BELIEVERS

YHWH intended the Gentiles to receive the same blessings as Israel but He has prescribed only one lifestyle for mankind to follow and it is that described in the Torah (Law) given at Mount Sinai. Just like Israel, the Gentile nations would be required to live the same Torah (Law) observant lifestyle. To receive the same level of reward would require the same level of commitment. It was and still is the same deal. To teach that the whole Torah (Law) given at Mount Sinai is for Israel alone is to say that only Israel was meant to be blessed. Does this sound logical of the One who said "All souls are mine?" YHWH created us all and does not wish to lose a single soul be it Jewish or not. In Malachi YHWH expresses His discern for those not observing the whole Torah (Law):

> "Therefore I have in turn made you contemptible and vile before all people, because you did not keep my ways but were partial in applying the Torah (Law)." (MALACHI 2:9)

A person can only keep His Ways by applying *all* that is in His Torah (Law), Genesis – Deuteronomy, in obedience to His edict in Deuteronomy 4.2 not to take anything away from that which He has given.

If, when Messiah Yeshua said, "Not one yud or stroke of the Torah (Law) will pass away," He was referring only to the Ten Commandments, why didn't He clarify this? Why didn't He inform His disciples that all of the other rulings given by the Father were about to become obsolete with His death? It is because such an eventuality would have contradicted the Father's decree in Deuteronomy 4:2 and was never part of the Father's plan. To shrink the Torah (Law) is to cause it to fade, to pass away. In His rebuke of the Pharisees in John, Messiah Yeshua actually confirms the continued relevance of the 'Books of Moses' until judgment:

> "But don't think that it is I who will be your accuser before the Father. Do you know who will accuse you? Moshe (Moses), the very one you have counted on. For if you believed Moshe, you would believe Me; because it was about Me that he wrote. But if you don't believe what he wrote, how are you going to believe what I say?" (JOHN 5:45)

In the Introduction it was explained that YHWH's Torah (Law) was commonly referred to as the 'Books of Moses' and Messiah Yeshua is here speaking in this context. In telling His audience they would be accused by Moses, Messiah Yeshua was speaking metaphorically. It is not Moses himself that is to judge but what he wrote down and gave to the nation — YHWH's Torah (Law). In other words all will be judged against their performance of YHWH's Torah (Law) as confirmed by Paul in Romans 2:13. This issue is discussed further under 'Colossians 2:14' later in this Part 3.

G) KEEPING TORAH (LAW) TODAY

It was shown in Part 1 of this book how compliance with the scriptures requires a full day of worship with respect to YHWH's Shabbats. Of all His Shabbats, YHWH knew that His weekly Shabbat would prove to be the most difficult for mankind to faithfully observe. This is most probably why the weekly Shabbat is the only Shabbat included in the Ten Commandments. However, Torah (Law) observance has to be understood in terms of today's society. It has to be acknowledged that YHWH's Torah (Law) was never meant for a situation such as exists today. The Torah (Law) was given to an entire community to be adopted at a national level as a national constitution. It was for this purpose that YHWH separated a complete race of people, intending for them to remain together in a specific location; 'in the land.' Ariel and D'vorah Berkowitz in their book, 'Torah Rediscovered' illustrate YHWH's intention by way of a map of Israel with the word 'Torah' repeated around the perimeter of the country and forming its border. Their illustration exactly portrays YHWH's original intention for the whole of the nation of Israel to be encapsulated under the umbrella of His Torah (Law). The efficacy of the Torah (Law) required its acceptance at a national level, which necessitated that every day life for the whole of the country be organized around YHWH's Torah (Law). Unfortunately everywhere, society today shows little interest in YHWH's Torah (Law) and far from encouraging a lifestyle commensurate with the Torah (Law), society today promotes the opposite. YHWH's weekly Shabbat has become the universally recognized day of sport and His annual Shabbats pass unrecognized by most. Commerce spans six if not seven days of the week and those who escape the snare of sport usually fall prey to the snare of work.

We live in a world today that promotes a lifestyle deliberately designed to compromise obedience to YHWH's Torah (Law). Life is forever wetting the appetite of the flesh, offering attractive alternatives tailored to dilute the will of the individual to keep Torah (Law). But we each have the freedom to chose, it is simply a question of what choice do we wish to make. If we feed the flesh we starve the Spirit. Difficult as it may be, it is not impossible to honour that which YHWH requires of us. Where obedience is a matter of choice there can be no excuse. He expects and is entitled to, our best efforts for obedience and to put Him first before all else.

This writer is friendly with a family having two daughters. This family devoutly honours YHWH's weekly and annual Shabbats. At the time of writing both daughters were in their teens, one seeking work and the other about to graduate from school. The parents have instilled upon their daughters a lifestyle obedient to Torah (Law). So successfully have they led their daughters that, coming to an age of independence, both daughters are demonstrating a willingness to sacrifice opportunities where such require contravention of YHWH's Torah (Law). One, although enthusiastically searching for employment refuses to consider employment which requires Saturday working. The other being a talented musician and having aspirations in this field has, for the sake of Torah (Law), rejected desirable opportunities. Doubtless there are others and such families are a wonderful example to us all. Living proof that all that is required is the will.

Remember Romans 2:13, ultimately each of us will be judged against the resolve we have shown towards YHWH's Torah (Law).

NEW COVENANT THEOLOGY

H) CHRISTIANITY'S MISCONCEPTION OF THE NEW COVENANT

Another teaching within Christianity is that believers are under a new covenant which has annulled or negated Elohim's Torah (Law). Such a belief makes little sense when we consider YHWH's Torah (Law) is the only means of maintaining a correct/pleasing relationship with Him and that the Hebrew word Torah does not mean law but teaching/instruction. By presenting the scriptures in two parts and labelling them Old Testament/Covenant and New Testament/ Covenant, the Church has complicated what are the covenants in the scriptures. The truth of the scriptures would be a lot clearer if they were not divided or labelled in this manner. Neither is there any good reason for such a division or labelling when we realise that Messiah Yeshua did *not* introduce any new covenant. The Son is the mediator of the Father's new covenant, (Hebrews 8:6, 9:15, 12:24). Messiah Yeshua's subservience to the Father is repeatedly revealed throughout the scriptures. Below are just a few examples where the Son Himself shows his obsequiousness to the Father, starting with Hebrews 10:5 where it repeats the Psalmist:

> This is why, on coming into the world, He says, "It has not been your will to have an animal sacrifice and a meal offering; rather, you have prepared for Me a body. No, you have not been pleased with burnt offerings and sin offerings. Then I said 'Look! In the scroll of the book it is written about Me, I have come to do your will.'"

The phrase, 'scroll of the book' is a reference to the Tanakh (Old Testament) which of course includes the Torah (Law). It should be remembered that it is the Father's plan of redemption for mankind, not the Son's. It is the Father's Torah (Law), the Father's Word not the Son's Word. Messiah Yeshua is fully obedient and subservient to His Father's will, He does not have a plan of His own, He is constantly reminding us of this when speaking of His return He says:

> "But when that day and hour will come no one knows — not the angels in heaven, not the Son, only the Father." (MATTHEW 24:36)

Messiah Yeshua tells us that He was sent by the Father:

> "Here's what the work of Elohim is; to trust in the One He sent." (JOHN 6:29)

Messiah Yeshua is executor of the Father's will, not of His own will:

> "For I have come down from heaven to do not My own will but the will of the One who sent Me." (JOHN 6:38)

It is the Father who is in control:

> "No one can come to Me unless the Father – the One who sent Me — draws him." (JOHN 6:44)
>
> "This," He said, "Is why I told you that no one can come to Me unless the Father has made it possible for him." (JOHN 6:65)

Messiah Yeshua pleads with His Father to take away His cup of suffering:

> "My Father, if possible, let this cup pass from Me; Yet — not what I want, but what you want." (MATTHEW 26:39)

Refer also Acts 1:6.

We need to remember what we have said earlier; at the time of Messiah Yeshua and the Apostles there was no two parts to the scriptures. All they had to refer to was the Tanakh what Christian bibles refer to as the 'Old Testament/Covenant.' Therefore, when either Messiah Yeshua or the Apostles make reference to both old and new covenants, their reference has to be associated with what is contained in the Tanakh. They cannot be referring to the second part of the scriptures, it did not exist. Messiah Yeshua would heed His Father's command — not to add to His Word, therefore He would not introduce a new covenant of His own. There cannot be two new covenants. So which are the covenants mentioned in the scriptures that Messiah Yeshua and the Apostles referred to as old and new?

I) THE OLD AND NEW COVENANTS IN THE SCRIPTURES

The only place in scripture where YHWH declares a new covenant is in Jeremiah:

> "Here, the days are coming," says YHWH, "when I will make a new covenant with the house of Israel and with the house of Y'hudah (Judah). It will not be like the covenant I made with their fathers on the day I took them by their hand and brought them out of the land of Egypt; because they, for their part, violated My covenant, even though I, for My part, was a husband to them," Says YHWH. "For this is the covenant I will make with the house of Israel after those days," says YHWH. "I will put My Torah (Law) within them and write it on their hearts; I will be their Elohim and they will be My people." (JEREMIAH 31:31–33)

In the whole of the scriptures these are the only verses introducing a new covenant and far from any annulment or negation, YHWH's Torah (Law) remains the whole basis of this new covenant. These verses define the old covenant as that given to the Israelite nation at Sinai during their exodus from Egypt. Notice also, as with the Sinai covenant, this new covenant only concerns the Israelite nation; the descendants of Abraham. It does not mention the Gentile nations.

J) THE DIFFERENCE BETWEEN THE OLD AND NEW COVENANTS

So what is the difference between the old and new covenants? As we have just said, YHWH's Torah (Law) is the basis of both covenants, there is no attempt at negation or annulment of YHWH's Torah (Law). One difference between the old and new covenants is explained in Ezekiel 36:26–27 where YHWH explains why a new covenant is necessary:

> "I will give you a new heart and put a new spirit inside you; I will take the stony heart out of your flesh and give you a heart of flesh. I will put My spirit inside you and cause you to live by My laws, respect My rulings and obey them." (EZEKIEL 36:26–27)

The problem with the old covenant was never its foundation; YHWH's Torah (Law) but the hearts of the people who received it. Theirs was a heart of stone and in Zechariah we are given a definition of what this term means:

> 'But they wouldn't listen, they stubbornly turned their shoulder away and stopped up their ears so that they wouldn't have to hear it. Yes, they made their hearts as hard as a diamond, so they wouldn't hear the Torah (Law) and the messages that YHWH had sent by His Spirit through the earlier prophets. This is why great anger came from YHWH.' (ZECHARIAH 7:11–12)

Because the people rebelled against His Torah (Law), YHWH describes them as having hearts as hard as diamond, which is of course stone. YHWH expresses His disdain over their hard heartedness in Deuteronomy:

> "Oh how I wish their hearts would stay like this always, that they would fear Me and obey all My mitzvot (commandments); so that it would go well with them and their children forever." (DEUTERONOMY 5:29)

A heart of stone is a heart that rejects YHWH's Torah (Law). Conversely, as can be understood from the above verses from Ezekiel, a heart of flesh is fully receptive of YHWH's Torah (Law) via the Ruach HaKodesh (HS) implanted within the person. It is the presence of YHWH's Spirit within us that helps overcome man's sinful nature inherited from Adam and characterised by the phrase 'heart of stone.'

A second and very substantial difference between the old and new covenants was described by Messiah Yeshua during His final meal with His disciples: we are told:

> Also He took a cup of wine, made the b'rakhah (gave thanks) and gave it to them, saying "All of you drink from it! For this is My blood, which ratifies the New Covenant, My blood shed on behalf of many, so that they may have their sins forgiven." (MATTHEW 26:27–28)

Messiah Yeshua does not say His blood is a new covenant rather, it ratifies the new covenant. Hence He is not introducing another covenant. Consequently, He could only be referring to the new covenant promised by His Father and spoken of in Jeremiah. The question is what effect has Messiah Yeshua's blood on the new covenant? The author of Hebrews provides the answer by way of his criticism of the old covenant:

> "For it is impossible that the blood of bulls and goats should take away sins." (HEBREWS 10:4)

According to this verse the old covenant system of animal sacrifice was unable, in his words, to 'take away' sins. By this statement the writer of Hebrews is differentiating between forgiveness of sin and taking away sin because there can be no doubt that forgiveness of sins was attainable under the old covenant system: Leviticus 4:20, 4:26, 4:31, 4:35, 5:10 and 15:28. There is however, a theology that all sins committed prior to Messiah Yeshua's coming were rolled over until His sacrifice. This 'roll over' concept does not agree with what is said concerning Yom Kippur (Day of Atonement) in the scriptures:

> 'For on this day, atonement will be made for you, to purify you; you will be clean before YHWH from all your sins.' (LEVITICUS 16:30)

This wording in no way infers a deferment of forgiveness. It says that the person could stand (present tense) clean before YHWH: atonement means atonement. An amplification of what is meant by the words 'to cleanse you' can be found in Hebrews 9:22. Here it confirms that the shedding of blood leads to the remission of sins. Remission means to be let off from punishment, as does forgiveness mean to give up the wish to punish or get even with. The sacrificial system was the means of reconciliation between the sinner and

YHWH, for the sinful act committed. In other words, through the sacrifice of the animal the sin was overlooked by YHWH and the sinner escaped punishment. But the sinful act was not forgotten, quite the contrary. Hebrews says of the old covenant sacrifices:

> 'In these sacrifices is a reminder of sins, year after year.' (HEBREWS 10:3)

On the other hand, YHWH says of His new covenant:

> "No longer will any of them teach his fellow community member or his brother, 'Know YHWH; for all will know Me, from the least of them to the greatest; because I will forgive their wickedness *and remember their sins no more.*'" (JEREMIAH 31:34)

These two scriptures provide an explanation for the phrase 'take way sins' in Hebrews. Contrary to the old covenant, under the new covenant sins will be completely blotted out as if they never existed. But this required a more perfect sacrifice; the sacrifice of Messiah Yeshua Himself and belief in the power of His sacrifice. The blood of Messiah Yeshua was integral to the new covenant promised in Jeremiah, making the new covenant prophetic of Messiah Yeshua's sacrificial death and His resurrection. It was in this knowledge that Messiah Yeshua spoke to His disciples in the way He did during His last meal with them.

The scriptures force upon us a new emphasis with respect to the forgiveness of sins under the new covenant when compared with the old covenant. Under the new covenant forgiveness, as spoken of by Messiah Yeshua during His exclamation to His disciples in Matthew 26:27–28, attaches the complete erasion of all sins committed. By His sacrifice Messiah Yeshua set us free from the bondage of sin, its hold over us was nailed to the stake forever:

> He entered the Holiest Place once and for all. And He entered not by means of the blood of goats and calves, but by means of His own blood, thus setting people free forever. (HEBREWS 9:12)

The efficacy of the new covenant is primarily dependant upon the two constituents: the blood (sacrifice) of Messiah Yeshua and the

Ruach HaKodesh (HS) of the Father. The resultant effect for all who partake of the new covenant is a pure (clean) conscience, (Hebrews 9:14). Compared with animal sacrifice which only achieved an outward purity, (Hebrews 9:13).

K) THE RELEVANCE OF ANIMAL SACRIFICE UNDER THE OLD COVENANT

Through the constant sacrifice of animals a person was continuously reminded of YHWH's Torah (Law) and his continuous transgressions. The system of animal sacrifice was an acknowledgement by the person offering the sacrifice that they had transgressed Elohim's Torah (Law) and thereby placed themselves outside of the whole community. Without this acknowledgement there is no recognition of the authority of the Torah (Law) and therefore, no respect for it. Without the sacrificial system sin would have continued unabated. The Torah (Law) would simply have disappeared and YHWH's concept of a holy community vanish with it. The sacrificial system was necessary to preserve the Torah (Law) and thereby preserve the concept of Israel being a holy (set apart) nation. Through the sacrifice of the animal a person was brought back under the umbrella of the Torah (Law) and back into the community.

L) THE NECESSITY FOR A NEW COVENANT

Earlier it was pointed out that the new covenant spoken of in Jeremiah refers only to the descendants of Abraham. This is better understood when we realise YHWH's reason for enacting a new covenant. YHWH made a promise with Abraham and all of his descendants:

> "I will be their Elohim and they will be My people."

To this promise YHWH added the promise of the land. These were everlasting covenants and any covenant made by the Creator of All must be kept. But YHWH can only work with righteous people and the only means of maintaining righteousness is obedience to His Torah (Law). Unfortunately Israel's sinful nature (stony heart) remains a permanent obstruction to YHWH's promise. For this reason the new covenant remains prophetic insofar as the nation of Israel is concerned, as substantiated in the following verses from Zechariah:

> "When that day comes, I will seek to destroy all nations attacking Yerushalayim (Jerusalem); and I will pour on the house of David and on those living in Yerushalayim (Jerusalem) a spirit of grace and prayer; and they will look to Me whom they pierced. They will mourn for Him as one mourns for an only son; they will be in bitterness on His behalf like the bitterness for a firstborn. When that day comes there will be a great mourning in Yerushalayim, mourning like that for Hadad Rimmon in the Megiddo valley. Then the land will mourn, each family by itself — the family of the house of David by itself and their wives by themselves; the family of the house of Natan by itself and their wives by themselves; the family of the house of Levi by itself and their wives by themselves; the family of the house of Shim'i by itself and their wives by themselves; all the remaining families, each by itself and their wives by themselves." (ZECHARIAH 12:9–13).

> "When that day comes, a spring will be opened for the house of David and the people living in Yerushalayim to cleanse them from sin and impurity. When that day comes." says YHWH, "I will cut off the very names of the idols from the land so that no one even remembers them any more." (ZECHARIAH 13:1–2)

It is clear from the first verses that the Israelite nation as a whole will not have a repentant heart until the return of Messiah Yeshua and He reveals to them His hands and feet. Then they will realise it was Him 2,000 years ago. This revelation will fill the whole Israelite nation with grief and remorse. Chapter 13 continues this theme explaining how a cleansing of both the people and the land will follow. Together these two chapters show a fully repentant nation living in a cleansed land. This will require the whole of the Israelite nation to have a mindful desire (heart of flesh) to live in obedience to YHWH's Torah (Law). But look at the opening phrase in chapter 13 — 'When that day comes' — which day? Chapter 13 is a continuation of what is said in the preceding chapter and chapter 12 is talking about the time of the return of Messiah. In essence these chapters in Zechariah are the fulfilment of the promise spoken in Jeremiah 31:31–33; which also contains the same phrase 'in that day' but it will not happen until Messiah's return. The new covenant is in many respects but as is explained below not all, prophetic.

Ezekiel chapter 37 also describes a rejuvenated Israelite nation but not until after the resurrection of Israel's dead (Ezekiel 37:12) and their king Messiah Yeshua is ruling over them (Ezekiel 37:24). These verses from Zechariah and Ezekiel confirm that the new covenant spoken of in Jeremiah will not be enacted, insofar as Israel the nation is concerned, until the time of Messiah's return.

Because Judaism has not yet identified the name of Yeshua with the pre-eminent role of Messiah for the nation of Israel, the Jewish people cannot enjoy the benefits of this pre-inaugural age of new covenant understanding, which precedes the 'Messianic Age,' afforded to those who carry the testimony of Yeshua and keep YHWH's Torah (Law). For this reason, the new covenant age which, in accordance with the Tanakh (Old Testament), must include all Israel, together with its rewards, remains prophetically future. Yet today there are some amongst the Jewish people who have embraced Yeshua and advance a proper Torah (Law) centered lifestyle. But the new covenant as spoken of by the prophets cannot come into completion until the dawn of the 'Messianic Age,' when all Israel enters into it on a national level. Messiah Yeshua was alluding to this fact when, referring to the cup of wine during His last meal with His disciples He said, He will not drink of it again until the reign of His Father, (Matthew 26:27–29). Messiah Yeshua was referring to His millenium reign. Not until He returns will Israel as a nation enter into the new covenant thereby enabling completion of the Abrahamic promise. This is the sole reason for His return and 1000 years rule. However, in recognition of today's gradual return of the Jewish people to their Elohim, the following is written in Hebrews in reflection of an age still to come:

> By using the term 'new,' He has made the first covenant 'old;' and something being made old, something in the *process of aging*, is on its way to vanishing altogether. (HEBREWS 8:13)

Not until the return of Messiah and His acceptance by the Jewish people as a whole, will portions of the old covenant be replaced by provisions of the new, thus rendering the old outdated portions obsolete. But it should be remembered that the new covenant was first mentioned only in terms of the nation of Israel as a whole.

M) SALVATION AND THE NEW COVENANT

When we consider that only the sacrifice of Messiah Yeshua is perfect enough to take away sin and amalgamate this with the words spoken by YHWH when referring to His new covenant: "I will forgive their wickedness and remember their sins no more," can there be any doubt that Messiah Yeshua was referring to His Father's covenant when He spoke of His blood during His last meal with His disciples? Messiah Yeshua's 'blood of the new covenant' provides an eternal inheritance in heaven and an eternal presence with our Father YHWH for all partakers of the new covenant:

> 'So brothers, we have confidence to use the way into the Holiest Place opened by the blood of Yeshua. He inaugurated it for us as a new and living way through the parokhet (curtain), by means of His flesh." (HEBREWS 10:19–20)

Add the exclamation of Messiah Yeshua in John 14:6:

> "I AM the Way — and the Truth and the Life, no one comes to the Father accept through Me."

These verses substantiate the removal of the separation existing between Israel and YHWH and inherent with the old covenant. Because animal sacrifice was unable to take away sin YHWH remained unapproachable behind the temple curtain. We are told that simultaneously with Messiah Yeshua's death there was an earthquake and the temple curtain, symbolising separation, was torn in two.

> "The Elohim of our fathers raised up Yeshua, whereas you men killed Him by having Him hanged on a stake. Elohim has exalted this man *at His right hand* as Ruler and Saviour, in order to enable Israel to do t'shuvah (repentance) and have her sins forgiven." (ACTS 5:30–31)

N) THE GENTILE NATIONS AND THE NEW COVENANT

All of the above is specific to the Israelite nation. So where does this leave the Gentile nations? What may not be appreciated is that whilst Messiah Yeshua walked the earth He never said or did anything to invite the Gentile nations into any covenant with Elohim. As we have said Messiah Yeshua did not make any covenants with anybody, this was the sole right of the Father as the Creator, not Messiah Yeshua. Whilst on earth Messiah Yeshua's only concern was for the Jewish people. He actually instructed his disciples to exclude the Gentiles:

> "Don't go into the territory of the Goyim (Gentiles) and don't enter any town in Shomron, but go rather to the lost sheep of the house of Israel." (MATTHEW 10:5–6)

Messiah Yeshua later reiterates that it is only the house of Israel that He is concerned with and actually rebuked a gentile woman who approached Him:

> A woman from Kena'an who was living there came to Him, pleading "Sir, have pity on me, Son of David! My daughter is cruelly held under the power of demons." But Yeshua did not say a word to her. Then His talmidim (disciples) came to Him and urged Him, Send her away, because she is following us and keeps pestering us with her crying. He said, "I was sent only to the lost sheep of the house of Israel." But she came, fell at His feat and said, "Sir help me!" He answered and said, "It is not right to take the children's food and toss it to their pet dogs." (MATTHEW 15:22–26)

So are the Gentile nations to be excluded by YHWH? This would be strange indeed considering His claim to all souls in Ezekiel. There are however, several scriptures in which Paul clarifies YHWH's intention for Gentiles. Let us first bring two such scriptures together:

> Therefore, remember your former state you Gentiles by birth – called the Uncircumcised by those who, merely because of an operation on their flesh are called the Circumcised – at that time had no messiah. You were estranged from the national life of Israel. You were foreigners to the covenants embodying Elohim's promise. You were in this world without hope and without Elohim. But now, you who were once far off have been brought near through the shedding of Messiah's blood. (EPHESIANS. 2:11–13)

> For in union with the Messiah, you are all children of Elohim through this trusting and faithfulness; because as many of you were immersed into the Messiah have clothed yourselves with the Messiah, in whom, there is neither Jew nor Gentile, neither slave nor freeman, neither male nor female, for in union with the Messiah Yeshua, you are all one. Also, if you belong to the Messiah, you are seed of Avraham (Abraham) and heirs to the promise. (GALATIANS 3:26–29)

Whilst the Gentiles are not a direct party to any covenant, old or new, those who have put their trust in atonement through Messiah Yeshua are *considered* as the seed of Abraham and become *heirs* to the promise. The impact of the above verses is to place all Gentile believers under the new covenant. Earlier we saw how, at the time of His humanity Messiah Yeshua excluded the Gentiles. Now look at the contrast in His instruction to His disciples after His ascension to heaven and the offering of His blood before the Father:

> "Therefore, go and make people from all nations into talmidim (disciples), immersing them into the reality of the Father, the Son and the Ruach HaKodesh (HS). (MATTHEW 28:19)

Paul further clarifies the Gentile position in Romans chapter 11. In these verses Paul describes the Jew/Gentile relationship using the analogy of two olive trees: a cultivated olive and a wild olive. Such an analogy is not surprising when we consider YHWH so often talks in terms of an olive tree when discussing Israel: Jeremiah 11:16, Psalms 52:8, 128:3. Isaiah 17:6, 24:13, Hos.14:5–6. Paul was very familiar with the Tanakh (Old Testament) and would be well aware of the imagery used by YHWH. It is clear from the terminology in his analogy that Paul designates Israel the cultivated tree and Gentiles the wild tree. Continuing, Paul then describes a grafting process that is rather strange. Contrary to the agricultural practice of grafting a cultivated branch into a wild olive, he describes the very opposite explaining how YHWH will take a wild branch (Gentile) and graft it into the cultivated tree (Israel). Here Paul could well be arguing, albeit prematurely, against replacement theology, that is, that the Church has replaced Israel as YHWH's covenant people. Surely if this was so would Paul not have described the grafting process in accordance with and not contrary to agricultural practice? It is for this reason that Paul reminds the recipients of his letter that the root supports them and not vice versa. Whatever you may consider the root to be; the Patriarchs, the Torah (Law) or Messiah Yeshua — it is a Jewish root. It is the Gentiles who inherit and not Israel. It is the covenant promise given to all Israel: "I will be their Elohim and they will be My people," that the Gentiles inherit. But with this is inherited the same covenant obligations, equal observance of His Torah (Law) as that required of Israel.

The essence of these verses in Romans is often lost due to controversy; arguments about what the tree is and what the root is. We need to focus on what Paul is telling us and not on that which he has not mentioned. The simple message here is that Gentiles are not excluded from YHWH's plan. As we said earlier in this book, the very reason Israel were selected by YHWH was to lead the Gentile nations to Him.

To conclude this section, Messiah Yeshua's sacrifice was the signature that YHWH is the Elohim of *all* mankind — available to all who want Him.

COLOSSIANS 2:14

With what we have learnt we are now in a position to revisit Colossians 2:14. Let us remind ourselves what this verse says;

> "Having wiped out the handwriting of requirements that was against us, which was contrary to us. And He has taken it out of the way, having nailed it to the cross" (NKJV)

As was previously pointed out under section D of this part 3, the interpretation promoted by some church leaders creates contention with what is said elsewhere in the scriptures and must therefore be erroneous. So what would be a more acceptable interpretation? First note what is said in Revelation:

> Next I saw a great white throne and the One sitting on it. Earth and heaven fled from His presence, and no place was found for them. And I saw the dead, both great and small, standing in front of the throne. Books were opened, and another book was opened; the Book of Life; and the dead were judged from what was written in the books, according to what they had done. (REVELATION 20:11–12)

In other words, judgment is a comparison between 'what a person has done' that is, the lifestyle he/she has live, compared with what is written in the 'books that were opened.' Revelation infers the existence of a handwritten heavenly record of the lifestyles of every man, woman and child that ever lived and spoken of in 2 Corinthians:

> "For we must all appear before the Messiah's court of judgment, where everyone will receive the good or bad consequences of what they did while they were in the body." (2 CORINTHIANS 5:10)

In this passage the phrase 'in the body' means in the flesh. This being the case consider the following abstraction:

- From revelation we may conclude that every individual's lifestyle has been recorded in a heavenly log, written by the hand of the heavenly host and all will be judged by what is written about them...
- In John's Gospel, Messiah Yeshua stated this judgment will be against the Books of Moses, refer to section F of this part 3. In other words how each individual's lifestyle compares with what YHWH instructed in His Torah (Law). A fact confirmed by Paul in Romans 2:13.
- With Messiah's death the believer's transgressions were blotted out, gone, forever forgiven. Refer Hebrews 9:12.

- Colossians 2:14 says, that which is written is nailed to the stake (cross).

Analysing the above, a believer's sins (defined as transgressions against the Torah – Books of Moses) and recorded by hand in a heavenly log, have been wiped out with Messiah Yeshua's death. In other words they have been nailed to the stake. To summarise, it is the hand written list of transgressions that Colossians 2:14 is describing as having been nailed to the stake, for all believers who have lived in accordance with YHWH's instruction: His Torah (Law). It is not the handwriting of Moses.

For further evidence of heavenly records see Hebrews 12:23.

CONCLUSION TO PART 3

YHWH is all about Torah, the Torah is the A to Z of YHWH and this cannot be over emphasized. His Torah is the only provision He has provided for the spiritual health of mankind. It is the only way to a proper relationship with Him and He has instructed for His Torah to remain exactly as given at Mount Sinai:

> 'Do not add to what I am saying and *do not subtract from it.*'
> (DEUTERONOMY 4:2,12:32, PROVERBS 30:5 & REVELATION 22:18)

These words of YHWH prevent any abridgement, deletion, addition or messaging *of any kind whatsoever* of His Word. Mankind is not at liberty to pick and chose which parts of the scriptures are applicable and which are not. Yet Christianity approaches YHWH's Torah with a 'hit and miss' mentality, willing to acknowledge part of the Torah such as that containing the Ten Commandments but little else. Remember YHWH's rebuke of the Israelites for their partial approach to His Torah:

> "Therefore I have in turn made you contemptible and vile before all the peoples, because you did not keep my ways but were *partial* in applying the Torah (Law)." (MALACHI 2:9)

Do Christians really believe they will get away with doing that for which Israel was rebuked? In James we are told:

> For a person who keeps the whole Torah (Law), yet stumbles at one point, has become guilty of breaking them all. (JAMES 2:10)

Throughout the Tanakh (Old Testament) we are told of Israel's failure to follow YHWH's Torah and of the consequences they suffered, in fact are still suffering, for their disobedience. Why do you think we have such a detailed and comprehensive record of these people in our scriptures? It is for one reason only, so that we will not make the same mistake. Obedience means complete obedience to *all* He has given, as confirmed by Messiah Yeshua's words that not one yud or stroke of the Torah will pass away until all is complete.

If a faith is Torahless, lawless (whether wholly or partially is irrelevant) it is a counterfeit faith and its god or messiah must also be counterfeit. In the Introduction to this book the reader was encouraged not to be awed by the magnitude of the deceit mankind is currently under. Revelation says the whole world worshipped the beast, in other words, the whole of mankind is following apostasy. The whole of mankind has either thrown away YHWH's rule book or torn some pages out of it and according to James 2:10 it doesn't matter which it is. Either has the effect of placing a person on the wrong side of YHWH. Do not be prejudiced by the size of the deceit, no matter what its magnitude, a deceit is still a deceit. What we have today is nothing less than the fulfilment of what is said in Revelation.

As individuals we must separate teaching from preaching. It is for each one of us to research the truth for ourselves. To test what we are told and not just accept what comes from a pulpit. True learning does not come from listening, it comes from reading. Time is very short, only one end time prophecy remains before the return of Messiah Yeshua; it is the prophesy contained within 2 Thessalonians 2: 3–11, that being:

- the truth is made known to mankind: this book
- Rejection of the truth by those whose names are not written in the Book of Life,
- Elohim's delusion for those in rejection: the counterfeit messiah,

- The tribulation for all mankind: counterfeit imposing a single religion with himself at its head,
- The 'falling away:' the whole of mankind, except for those whose names are written in the Book of Life, following the counterfeit,
- Elohim's wrath: 'The Day of YHWH.'

Although the following words were spoken millennia ago — what has changed?

> "But you shall say to them, 'This is a nation that did not obey the voice of YHWH their Elohim, nor did they accept instruction (Torah). Truth has perished and has been cut off from their mouth.'" (JEREMIAH 7:28) (TS)

In closing, there is a lot said in the church about a rapture. Christians believe they will be taken up to meet their messiah in the air. But Christians will not meet the true Messiah Yeshua because He has no relationship with them:

> "Their worship of Me is useless, because they teach man made rules as if they were doctrines." (MATTHEW 15:9)

They are worshiping Him in vain, following the traditions of man — Christmas, Easter, Sunday worship and discarded YHWH's designated times decreed in Leviticus 23. Christianity is lawless (Torahless) and remember what Messiah Yeshua says of the lawless in Matthew 7:21:

> "Not everyone who says to Me, 'Master, Master!' will enter the Kingdom of Heaven, only those who do what My Father in heaven wants. On that Day, many will say to Me, 'Master, Master! Didn't we prophesy in your name? Didn't we expel demons in your name? Didn't we perform miracles in your name?' Then I will tell them to their faces. 'I never knew you! Get away from Me you workers of lawlessness."

Remember your lifestyle will be judged against the 'Books of Moses; YHWH's Torah.

This book has presented to you only what is said in the scriptures. The content of this book is all factual there is nothing illusory. The writer urges Christians to seriously contemplate what is revealed in this book and to shake off the shackles of apostate church theology. Remember your destiny is always in your own hands. When your judgment comes it will be no defence to say we were misled because now you have read the truth. Now you will have no excuse when you stand in front of Messiah Yeshua.

A BULLET FROM HEAVEN

PART FOUR

PART FOUR

Epilogue

PART 1

We are told that at the beginning man was created in the image of Elohim, that is, man was created righteous. Man was created sinless but not just man, the whole of creation was sinless. Elohim is perfect and all He does is perfect, therefore His creation as created by Him was perfect. All was created in Elohim's realm, the eternal realm of immortality. We are told that Elohim was pleased with what He had created, so why would He sentence His creation, which was pleasing to Him, to a definite life span and an eventual death?

When sin entered creation through disobedience, creation was catapulted out of Elohim's realm; the eternal realm and into the realm of time. Death marks time and death is the reward of sin. All creation now has a life span. Everything rots in its own time, and everything eventually dies. Paul tells us in 1 Corinthians 15:50–54 that the mortal cannot enter that which is immortal. Through the disobedience of Adam and Eve sin entered creation and took creation away from YHWH and out of His realm.

Ever since the disobedience of Adam and Eve, mankind has continued to spiral further and further away from the one who created them: YHWH. Today YHWH's holy day has become the primary day for sport. Schools and clubs alike are teaching young children to ignore YHWH's commandment to keep the Saturday Shabbat holy. Indeed the leaders themselves of most of these institutions are most likely ignorant of the true Shabbat day and the principle behind it as disclosed in part 1 of this book. In many ways the situation existing today parallels that which existed before the great flood:

> The earth also was corrupt before Elohim, and the earth was filled with violence. Elohim saw the earth and yes, it was corrupt, for all living beings had corrupted their ways on the earth. (GENESIS 6:11)

Mankind is not keeping the instructions given by YHWH in Sinai over 3000 years ago. Instruction given to the Israelite nation for the benefit of all mankind. Not a single law has ever been rescinded. But man has negated, annulled and distorted that which YHWH decided was necessary. YHWH is perfect, all He does is perfect; therefore His Torah (Law) as given by Him is perfect. That is why Messiah confirmed that 'not one jot or tittle of the Torah (Law) will fade. Perfection needs no alteration, no change.

Let me repeat what I said earlier, most will reject this book. At the time of the great flood only eight people from the whole of mankind were deemed righteous and so only one righteous family was saved: proof YHWH is concerned with righteousness not numbers. If today He can find only eight people righteous enough for salvation, then He is no worse off than at the time of Noah. Eight people from the whole of the population of the world, what a sad testament that would be for mankind. But sad or not, YHWH will not bend His rules. Righteousness is accredited only to those who keep His Torah (Law) as given at Sinai and not as distorted by man. Today the whole world is following a false teaching. This state of mankind will remain until YHWH's intervention. According to scripture very few will accept the truth, as is contained in this book, For them, this book will indeed prove to be — a bullet from heaven, the choice is with you.

PART 2

The following are a few additional verses from scripture pertinent to the subject matter of this book. They are by no means the only relevant verses and are provided here as a guide memoire. The verses have not been arranged in the order of the scriptures but in a manner considered to provide a better correlation with the issue of this book — YHWH's truth.

Isaiah 24:5:

> The land lies defiled under its inhabitants because they have transgressed the teachings, changed the law and broken the everlasting covenant.

Although this verse is a direct reference to Israel's disobedient behaviour, do you think the Gentile nations who have committed the same offenses will be considered differently? Remember we all wish to be heirs of the same promise (Galatians 3:26), that is, I will be their Elohim and they will be My people. But YHWH gave one set of rules for the enactment of this promise — His Torah (Law).

Isaiah 29:13:

> And YHWH said, "Because these people approach Me with empty words and the honour they bestow on Me is mere lip service, while in fact they have distanced their hearts from Me, and their 'fear of Me' is just a mitzvot (commandment) of human origin.'

Unless you worship YHWH in the manner He prescribed your worship is empty. By ignoring His Torah (Law) you distance yourself from Him. Following the traditions of man: Easter, Christmas, Sunday worship etc, is obeying the commandments of men: commandments of human origin.

Isaiah 2:22:

> Stop relying on man in whose nostrils is a mere breath – after all he doesn't count for much, does he?

Christians need to stop accepting the false preaching promoting man made changes to the Torah (Law) of Elohim.

Jeremiah 17:5:

> Here is what YHWH says, "A curse on the person who trusts in humans, who relies on merely human strength."

When we compare that which YHWH promised Israel in Leviticus chapter 26 if they chose the path of disobedience; pestilence, wars, crop failure, famine, and starvation with the world situation today, can there be any doubt where mankind is in YHWH's eyes?

Isaiah 1:28:

> 'Rebels and sinners together will be broken and those who abandon YHWH will be consumed.'

You cannot separate YHWH from His Torah (Law) because the rules *He has given* are the only means of maintaining a proper relationship with Him. By abandoning His Torah (Law) you abandon Him. The scriptures are very clear — it is YHWH's way or no way. There is no room for man's deviation.

PART 3

When one considers how deeply rooted and universal false religious teaching is today, coupled with mankind's inherent willingness to close its eyes to the truth, one has to question just how effective this book will be. This book is certainly not going to destroy Papal Rome or Christianity. Scripture shows they will be present when the counterfeit is released from the abyss and form the matrix for his end time apostasy. The book of Revelation confirms that it is divine intervention that will ultimately rid the world of its universal apostasy. This book will however identify those whose names are written in the Book of Life. These are they for whom this book will prove to be a life changing experience. But how are they to continue with worship and learning? If they are members of a congregation identified by this book as lawless (Torahless) and which refuses to change, then they need to extract themselves from that congregation. There are congregations that follow the truth of the scriptures and observe YHWH's Torah (Law) as He intended. The reader is encouraged to find such a group. If no such congregation is available then they must join or even form, a home group with like minded people. The writer understands the initial difficulties this may propose and recommends prayer, YHWH will always support those seeking righteousness in His sight.

The following is a short list of recommended reading and course literature. However, the reader is put on guard: unfortunately even some authors who are on the right path fall foul of the mistake of using the name Jesus Christ for Messiah Yeshua. Hopefully these authors will correct this situation in all future works. Nonetheless, the content of their books is still valuable for developing further the revelations contained herein and learning more truth.

TITLE	**AUTHOR**
BOOKS	
Torah Rediscovered	Ariel & D'vorah Berkowitz
Your People Shall Be My People	Don Finto
Fellow Heirs	Tim Hegg
Galations	Avi Ben Mordechai
Come Out Of Her My People	C.J. Koster
Walk in the Light Series	Todd D Bennett
COURSES OF STUDY	
First Fruits Of Zion Inc.	First Fruits Of Zion Inc.
Chut HaM'shulash	Uri Marcus

Those who are in agreement with what is written in this book are encouraged to obtain a copy of scripture which is more aligned with the Hebrew roots of faith. Examples of such scriptures are The Complete Jewish Bible by David Stern and The Scriptures by the Institute for Scripture Research.

Qodesh Books are one source for obtaining recommended reading material. Their contact particulars are www.qodeshbooks.com.

Index

BARCHU ET YHWH HAM'VORACH LE-OLAM VA-ED
BLESS THE MASTER OF BLESSINGS FOREVER

ASHER NATAN LANU TORAT EMET
YOU HAVE GIVEN US THE TORAH OF TRUTH

VE'CHAYEI OLAM NATAH B'TOCHEINU
AND ETERNAL LIFE YOU HAVE PLANTED WITHIN US

BARUCH ATAH YHWH
BLESS YOU MASTER

NOTEIN HA-TORAH
GIVER OF THE TORAH

CPSIA information can be obtained at www.ICGtesting.com
Printed in the USA
LVOW011537280513

335806LV00021B/1048/P